Home
Bake
Eric Lanlard

To my mum, Louisette, and to my grandmother, Camille, who both taught me the importance of home cooking.

An Hachette UK Company
www.hachette.co.uk

First published in Great Britain in 2010 by Mitchell Beazley,
an imprint of Octopus Publishing Group Limited,
Endeavour House, 189 Shaftesbury Avenue, London, WC2H 8JY
www.octopusbooks.co.uk

First published in paperback in 2015

ISBN 978-1-78472-033-9

A CIP catalogue record for this book is available from the
British Library.

Printed and bound in China

10 9 8 7 6 5 4 3 2 1

Commissioning Editor: Rebecca Spry
Senior Art Editor: Juliette Norsworthy
Designer: Jaz Bahra
Photographer: Craig Robertson
Project Editor: Georgina Atsiaris
Editor: Susan Fleming
Home Economist: Rachel Wood
Prop Stylist: Morag Farquhar
Proofreader: Jo Richardson
Production Manager: Pete Hunt
Indexer: Vanessa Bird

Set in Glypha and Ropsenscript

**All eggs are medium free-range, unless otherwise stated
in the recipe.**

Home Bake

Eric Lanlard

641.86

MITCHELL BEAZLEY

Contents

Introduction

I am often asked what made me become a pâtissier, and where my love of baking came from. Neither my parents nor any of my relatives were in the profession, but as a child I was surrounded by food. If during the week our meals were simple, the weekend would turn into a culinary odyssey. Every Saturday my mum would prepare the most amazing lunch. She would go to a lot of trouble finding new recipes and no two Saturday meals were ever the same. Looking back, I really appreciate the effort that went into those weekend feasts! Of course, there was always a cake involved, and I remember fondly those beautiful tarts, gâteaux and loaves that came out of the oven – and the delicious aroma that met you when you entered the house. It was even more exciting when we went to stay with my grandmother, Mamie Camille, as we would go shopping at the market first thing in the morning to pick the best seasonal ingredients. My sister, Christine, and I would pretend that we were cooking for some fabulous manor house or castle!

So, yes, my family inspired me with their love of food and entertaining. As I started to experiment with recipes – from the age of six – I fell in love with the ingredients, the creativity and the techniques involved in making delicious and beautiful cakes. I learned quickly that you needed discipline, the right equipment and patience if you wanted to succeed. All of this was confirmed when I started my apprenticeship at the age of 18. I thought I knew it all and wanted to make the most ambitious pieces possible. I was reminded, however, that I should learn the basics first in order to understand how it all worked before moving on to bigger challenges.

Baking is not like regular cooking and this is where most people fail. If you don't know enough about the ingredients and how they interact with each other, you can experience disaster. To avoid this, you should always read and follow the instructions in the recipes, but of course, there is a big difference between home baking and the fine cakes that adorn pâtisserie windows. Home baking should be accessible, enjoyable and rewarding and, most importantly, stress-free. It is a perfect way in which to entertain the kids and teach them about good-quality food and the benefits of cooking at home. And you have the satisfaction of presenting fantastic desserts and cakes for every occasion.

In this book I introduce you to my favourite home-baking recipes, the ones I use at home when I entertain my family and friends, when I want to treat somebody or just because I feel like doing something different from what I produce at work. Baking is enjoying a huge revival, and with these straightforward recipes and multiple variations, you will be able to create delicious treats and become popular with your family and friends. But remember, follow the recipes carefully, only buy the best ingredients and, primarily, enjoy yourself!

Happy baking!

Eric

Sponge cakes

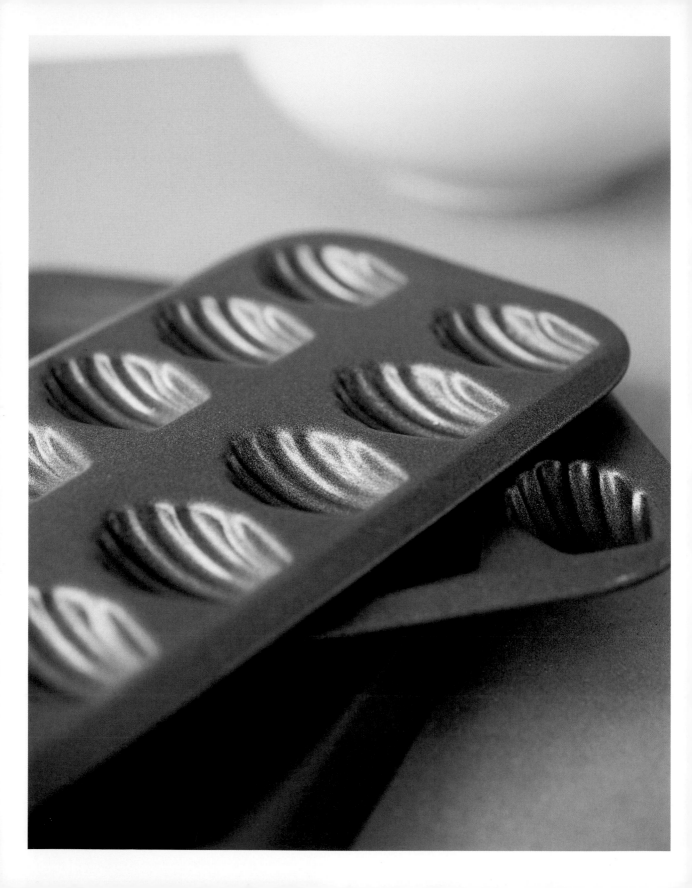

Sponge cakes

A good sponge should have a very light and airy texture. This is achieved by either beating the eggs and sugar to a foam, or by incorporating whipped egg white into the cake mixture. The principal technique of sponge-making involves retaining all this lovely air in the mixture when adding the flour or other dry ingredients.

These lovely, moist sponges are delicious on their own, or filled with creams, fresh fruits or home-made curds or preserves. They keep very well in airtight containers or old-fashioned cake tins. The fridge is usually a no-no, as this makes sponges harder and tighter in texture.

There are a few rules that should be followed for success. Firstly, all of the ingredients should be at room temperature before you start. Adding fridge-cold eggs to the butter and sugar mixture will result in it curdling, making the cake more dense. And once you have combined the dry and wet ingredients, put your cake in the oven straightaway, as the baking powder will start to do its job immediately; it will be less effective if it is left for a period of time before being cooked. I would also advise you to buy an oven thermometer, because ovens vary in temperature quite dramatically.

Make sure your ingredients are fresh. Once you have opened baking powder or self-raising flour, keep it for no longer than a month. After that, both will begin to lose their effectiveness, so your cakes won't rise properly. Almonds and spices should also be kept open for no longer than a month, unless they are stored in airtight containers.

Classic 'Cake Boy' chocolate sponge

I sell this in my London-based cafe-pâtisserie, Cake Boy. I always use melted chocolate in chocolate sponge recipes; I find cocoa powder less rich and tasty.

Serves 6
Preparation time: 20 minutes
Cooking time: 35 minutes

150g (5oz) unsalted butter, softened, plus
    extra for greasing
150g (5oz) good-quality dark chocolate,
    broken into pieces
150g (5oz) caster sugar
5 eggs
150g (5oz) self-raising flour
1 tsp baking powder

Preheat the oven to 180°C (fan 160°C)/350°F/gas mark 4. Grease a 20cm (8in) round sandwich tin with extra butter, and base-line with baking paper.

Put the chocolate pieces in a heatproof bowl that fits over a pan of gently simmering water (the base must not touch the water), and stir until it melts. Leave to cool slightly.

Meanwhile, cream the butter and sugar together in a large bowl, using an electric hand whisk on a medium-high speed, until light and fluffy. Lightly beat the eggs and gradually whisk them in until creamy and well combined. Sift the flour and baking powder into the bowl, and fold these in gently, using a large metal or rubber spatula. Finally, fold in the melted chocolate. You should have a smooth mixture.

Pour the mixture into the prepared tin, smooth the top and bake in the preheated oven for 35 minutes or until a metal skewer inserted into the centre comes out clean. Turn out on to a wire rack and peel away the paper. Leave to cool.

This sponge cake tastes wonderful filled with buttercream (see page 120) or ganache.

1

2

6

8

9

10

3

4

5

7

11

12

Classic 'Cake Boy' vanilla sponge

This is a more traditional sponge recipe for making a Victoria sandwich cake. It is not as light as the Genoise (see page 18), but works better as a tea-time cake than a dessert cake. It's another favourite at my cafe-pâtisserie, Cake Boy.

Serves 6
Preparation time: 20 minutes
Cooking time: 18–20 minutes

175g (6oz) unsalted butter, softened, plus extra for greasing
175g (6oz) golden caster sugar
1½ tsp vanilla extract
3 eggs
175g (6oz) self-raising flour
1 tsp baking powder

Preheat the oven to 180°C (fan 160°C)/350°F/gas mark 4. Grease two 18cm (7in) sandwich tins with extra butter, and base-line each with baking paper.

Cream the butter and sugar together in a large bowl, using an electric hand whisk on a medium-high speed, until light and fluffy. Add the vanilla extract and gradually beat in the eggs until creamy and well combined. Sift the flour and baking powder into the bowl, and fold everything together gently using a large metal spoon. You should have a light and fluffy mixture.

Divide the mixture between the prepared tins and smooth the tops. Bake in the preheated oven for 18–20 minutes until they are well risen and spring back when lightly pressed. Leave to cool in the tins for 5 minutes, then turn out on to a wire rack and peel away the paper. Leave to cool completely.

This sponge is delicious filled with lemon curd (for home-made see Tip page 138) or freshly whipped double cream and seasonal berries. It is also great to use in a dessert, such as the chocolate and cherry teardrops on page 200, or the salted butter caramel mousse with mini pears on page 190.

Tip

When adding the eggs, the cake mixture can look as if it has split. Don't panic – a teaspoon of flour stirred in will bring back smoothness to the cake mixture.

Mocha and roasted walnut sponge

I just love this recipe: it's perfect for an afternoon tea or picnic. You must make sure you use good-quality walnuts, though, as some of the cheap ones are bitter.

Serves 6
Preparation time: 20 minutes
Cooking time: 25 minutes

For the cake
225g (8oz) unsalted butter, softened,
    plus extra for greasing
225g (8oz) caster sugar
4 eggs
225g (8oz) self-raising flour
50g (2oz) pure cocoa powder
50g (2oz) lightly oven-roasted walnuts,
    roughly chopped
50g (2oz) oven-roasted coffee beans,
    roughly chopped
100ml (3½fl oz) espresso or strong coffee

For the coffee buttercream
250g (9oz) unsalted butter, softened
200g (7oz) icing sugar
4 tbsp very strong coffee (made with
    4 tsp instant coffee), cooled

Tip

When a recipe uses nuts or coffee beans, maximise the flavour by roasting in an oven preheated to 180°C (fan 160°C)/350°F/gas mark 4 for 5 minutes. This will intensify the flavour and they will keep their crunch for longer.

Preheat the oven to 170°C (fan 150°C)/325°F/gas mark 3. Grease two 20cm (8in) cake tins with extra butter, and base-line each with baking paper.

Cream the butter and sugar together in a large bowl using an electric hand whisk on a medium-high speed, until creamy and well combined. Add the eggs, one at a time, still whisking. Sift the flour and cocoa powder on to the mixture and fold in gently using a large metal spoon. Carefully mix in the walnuts and coffee beans so that they are evenly distributed. Pour in the coffee and stir until it is thoroughly combined.

Pour the cake batter into the prepared cake tins, and smooth the tops. Bake in the preheated oven for 25 minutes or until a metal skewer inserted into the centre comes out clean. When the cakes are cooked, remove from the oven and allow to cool in the tins for 10 minutes. Then remove them from the tins, peel away the paper and transfer them to a wire rack to cool completely to room temperature.

To make the coffee buttercream, place the softened butter and icing sugar in a bowl and, using an electric hand whisk, whisk until the butter is light, fluffy and almost white in colour. Then pour in the cooled coffee and whisk into the buttercream.

Put one of the cakes on to a plate, spread half the buttercream on to it, then put the other cake on top. Spread the remaining buttercream over the top. I like to decorate my cake with chocolate-coated coffee beans (available from any good deli) and walnut halves.

This cake should be eaten at room temperature so that all the flavours and the creaminess can be fully appreciated.

Plain Genoise sponge

This is the classic recipe that every pâtissier in France will use to make a fresh fruit gâteau or filled sponge. It is light with a lovely texture, and I like the nice rich colour compared to the whiteness of traditional sponge. I grew up on these cakes!

Serves 6
Preparation time: 20 minutes
Cooking time: 25 minutes

50g (2oz) unsalted butter, melted, plus
    extra for greasing
250g (9oz) plain flour, plus extra
    for dusting
250g (9oz) golden caster sugar
8 eggs

Preheat the oven to 180°C (fan 160°C)/350°F/gas mark 4. Grease two 22cm (8½in) sandwich tins with extra butter, and dust lightly with extra flour.

Put the sugar and eggs in a large heatproof bowl and set the bowl over a pan that is half-filled with gently simmering water. Using an electric hand whisk at full speed, whisk together continuously until hot. This will take about 10 minutes. The mixture will double in volume and should create a 'ribbon' effect (see Tip below) when it drops from the whisk. Remove the bowl from the pan of hot water.

Sift the flour on to the egg mixture, and fold it in gently with a large metal spoon, followed by the melted butter. Be careful not to over-mix!

Divide the mixture between the prepared tins, smooth the tops and bake in the preheated oven for about 25 minutes until golden in colour or when a metal skewer inserted into the centre comes out clean. Turn out on to a wire rack to cool.

This sponge will keep very well wrapped in clingfilm and it freezes well too. I prefer to cook my Genoise the day before I need it, as it is much easier to slice and work with.

Tip

The phrases 'to the ribbon' or 'ribbon effect' describe an important stage reached in mixing. When the spoon or beater is lifted out of the bowl, the mixture falls back into the bowl, like a satin ribbon. It will also leave a trail on the surface of the mixture.

Banana cake

For this recipe I use overripe bananas. They give a much better flavour than underripe or just-ripe fruit. My friend Laury from LA always makes this delicious loaf for brunch. She toasts slices under the grill with a large dusting of golden icing sugar, then serves them with maple syrup and fresh Greek yoghurt. Yum!

Serves 8
Preparation time: 20 minutes
Cooking time: 1 hour

125g (4½oz) unsalted butter, softened,
    plus extra for greasing
175g (6oz) unrefined soft brown sugar
2 eggs
300g (11oz) plain flour
1 tsp bicarbonate of soda
150ml (5fl oz) milk
3 medium very ripe bananas, peeled
    and mashed
1 tsp vanilla extract
1 tsp poppy seeds
75g (2¾oz) walnut halves, chopped
50g (2oz) dried banana chips

Preheat the oven to 180°C (fan 160°C)/350°F/gas mark 4. Lightly grease a 25 x 11cm (10 x 4¼in) loaf tin with extra butter.

Cream the butter and the sugar together in a large bowl using an electric hand whisk, until smooth. Add one of the eggs and beat in well, then add the second and continue to beat well. Sift in half the flour with the bicarbonate of soda, and mix well. Mix in the milk, then the remaining flour.

Fold the mashed bananas into the mixture along with the vanilla extract, poppy seeds and walnuts. Then tip the mixture into the loaf tin and level the top with a spatula. Arrange the banana chips on top of the mixture.

Bake in the preheated oven for around 1 hour until a skewer inserted in the centre comes out clean and not sticky. Cover the top with foil if it starts to brown too quickly.

Allow to cool in the tin for at least 20 minutes before turning out. To serve, cut into thick slices and serve warm or at room temperature.

Carrot cake

This all-American classic is such a versatile recipe: you can make it as a loaf, in a round or square baking tin or as a tray bake. Our US cousins use oil in a lot of their recipes and this gives you a very moist cake. Use a very dry cream cheese to give you nice firm frosting.

Serves 8
Preparation time: 30 minutes
Cooking time: 1½ hours

For the cake
unsalted butter, for greasing
225g (8oz) self-raising flour, plus extra
    for dusting
250ml (9fl oz) sunflower or corn oil
225g (8oz) golden caster sugar
3 large eggs
1 tsp ground cinnamon
1 tsp freshly grated nutmeg
250g (9oz) carrots, peeled
100g (3½oz) golden sultanas
100g (3½oz) walnut halves, chopped

For the frosting
300g (11oz) half-fat cream cheese
150g (5oz) unsalted butter, at room
    temperature
25g (1oz) unrefined golden icing sugar
1 orange

Tip

When whisking oil and sugar together, do not expect it to fluff up – you will not incorporate air into the mixture. This means that when you add the flour you can beat it in, as there is no air to lose.

Preheat the oven to 180°C (fan 160°C)/350°F/gas mark 4. Grease a rectangular loaf tin, 25 x 11cm (10 x 4¼in), with butter and dust with extra flour. Line the tin with baking paper.

Pour the oil into a large bowl. Add the caster sugar and mix with a large whisk for a few minutes. Add the eggs and beat. Rest a sieve over the bowl and tip in the flour plus the spices. Push the spiced flour through the sieve with a spoon. Using a large metal spoon, fold the flour into the egg mix until well combined.

Cut the ends off the carrots, then coarsely grate them. Fold the grated carrot, sultanas and walnuts into the mixture, ensuring that they are evenly distributed.

Pour it all into the prepared tin and spread evenly. Bake in the preheated oven for 1½ hours until well risen and golden, and a metal skewer inserted into the centre comes out clean. Cover the top with foil if it starts to brown too quickly. Leave to cool in the tin for 5 minutes, then turn out on to a wire rack to cool completely. Remove the paper.

Meanwhile, for the frosting, put the cream cheese and butter into a bowl and mix with a wooden spoon until soft and smooth. Put a sieve over the bowl and add the icing sugar, pushing it through with a spoon. Grate the orange against the fine side of a grater, stopping when you get to the white pith. Add this zest to the cream cheese frosting and mix well.

When the cake is cold, using a palette knife, spread a generous layer of the frosting on the top. Decorate if you like with a few extra sultanas and walnuts.

This cake will keep very well in a tin. Do not put it in the fridge, as it will go hard.

Lime and lemon drizzle cake

This is a perfect summer cake: it's delicious on its own, but equally yummy served with fresh berries and crème fraîche for a lazy alfresco lunch.

Serves 6
Preparation time: 15 minutes
Cooking time: 50 minutes

For the sponge
175g (6oz) unsalted butter, softened, plus extra for greasing
175g (6oz) golden caster sugar
3 large eggs
4 tbsp milk
225g (8oz) self-raising flour
finely grated zest of 1 lime and 1 lemon

For the sugar syrup drizzle
200g (7oz) icing sugar
juice of 2 limes and 2 lemons

For the decoration
finely grated zest of 1 lime and 1 lemon

Preheat the oven to 180°C (fan 160°C)/350°F/gas mark 4. Grease a 22cm (8½in) sandwich tin with extra butter, and base-line with baking paper.

To make the sponge, cream the butter and sugar together in a large bowl using an electric hand whisk, until they are pale and fluffy. Add the eggs, one at a time, still whisking. Once all the eggs have been added, pour in the milk and whisk to combine. Sift the flour on to the mixture, and fold it and the grated citrus zest gently into the mixture using a large metal spoon.

Turn the mixture into the prepared sandwich tin, smooth the top, and bake in the preheated oven for 50 minutes or until a skewer inserted into the centre comes out clean. Leave to cool on a wire rack for 10 minutes while still in the tin, then carefully turn out of the tin, remove the paper and leave to cool completely.

To prepare the sugar syrup drizzle, mix the icing sugar and citrus juices together well.

When the cake is cool, make tiny holes all over the top of the cake with a skewer. Gently pour the syrup over the top and into the holes until it is absorbed and starts to form a nice white crust.

Finely grate lemon and lime zest over the top of your cake, and serve.

Tip

This is a terrific cake to make the day before you want to eat it, as the sugar syrup drizzle will sink into the cake and make it taste even better the next day.

1

2

3

4

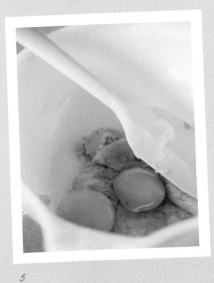

5

6

Madeleines

When I was young I would go with my mother to pâtisseries where they sold freshly baked madeleines from big glass jars.

Makes 20
Preparation time: 20 minutes
Cooking time: 10 minutes

90g (3¼oz) unsalted butter, plus
    2 tbsp melted unsalted butter for
    greasing
90g (3¼oz) plain flour, plus
    extra for dusting
2 tsp clear honey
40g (1½oz) icing sugar, plus extra
    for dusting
1 tsp baking powder
2 eggs
1 tsp orange-blossom water

Preheat the oven to 180°C (fan 160°C)/350°F/gas mark 4. Prepare a 20-hole madeleine mould by brushing with the melted butter. Get in there and make sure you reach all the ridges. Dust with flour and invert the pan, tapping out any excess flour.

Melt the butter and the honey together in a small saucepan, and leave to cool. Sift the flour, icing sugar and baking powder together into a large bowl. Stir in the cooled butter and honey mixture. Add the eggs and stir in, taking care not to over-mix. Fold in the orange blossom water.

Spoon the batter into the moulds, filling each mould two-thirds to three-quarters full. Bake the madeleines in the preheated oven for about 10 minutes or until risen and golden. Leave to cool for several minutes before turning out on to a wire rack and allowing to become completely cold.

Alternatives

Lemon: use the finely grated zest of 1 large lemon to replace the orange-blossom water.

Lemon thyme: strip the leaves off a few lemon thyme sprigs (the leaves are so small, they can be used whole) and add to the batter mixture after the butter. This will give a lovely fresh flavour.

Lime and honey: replace 25g (1oz) of the sugar with some extra clear honey and add the finely grated zest of 1 lime to the batter.

Pistachio: replace 25g (1oz) of the sugar with 25g (1oz) pistachio paste. Sprinkle some peeled chopped pistachios on top of the madeleines before putting in the oven.

Chocolate: you can dip your baked madeleines in melted dark chocolate too!

Tip

The old-fashioned metal tins give a better result than silicone ones when making madeleines.

Apple crumble sponge

This winning combination of two of my favourite hot puddings – apple crumble and hot baked sponge – is best served warm with vanilla custard.

Serves 6
Preparation time: 25 minutes
Cooking time: 35 minutes

For the sponge
100g (3½oz) unsalted butter, softened,
    plus extra for greasing
100g (3½oz) golden caster sugar
2 eggs
100g (3½oz) self-raising flour
1 tsp ground cinnamon
1 tsp baking powder
1 tsp vanilla extract
4 large Cox's apples

For the crumble
125g (4½oz) plain flour
50g (2oz) soft brown sugar
50g (2oz) unsalted butter, softened
½ tsp ground cinnamon
50g (2oz) rolled oats

To serve
runny honey

Preheat the oven to 180°C (fan 160°C)/350°F/gas mark 4. Grease a 22cm (8½in) springform cake tin with extra butter, and line with baking paper.

For the sponge, cream the butter and the sugar together in a large bowl, using an electric hand whisk at a medium-high speed. When nice and fluffy, add the eggs, one at a time, still beating. When the eggs are incorporated, sift on the flour, cinnamon and baking powder. Fold gently in, using a large metal spoon, then add and fold in the vanilla extract.

Spoon into the prepared springform tin, and smooth it out so that it is level. Peel and core the apples, cut them into nice fine slices and place them on top of the mixture. Make sure you leave a gap between them and the edges of the tin.

For the crumble, place all the crumble ingredients except the oats in a food processor and process briefly until you have a rough crumb mixture. Transfer the mixture to a bowl and stir in the oats until well combined. (I like my crumble chunky, so on purpose leave larger bits and pieces: they give a pleasing rustic look and are nice and crunchy when eating.)

Scatter the top of the sponge generously with the crumble. Bake in the preheated oven for 35 minutes. Leave to stand for 5 minutes, then remove the sides of the tin and peel away the paper. Put the cake on a serving dish and serve with runny honey for people to dribble over.

I love serving this cake warm with a hot Calvados-flavoured custard (see Tip page 196) when I've got adults eating at home; a perfect autumn indulgence.

Alternative

Pear or apricot: You can change the apples to the same weight of pears or apricots. The pears should be prepared in the same way as the apples; the apricots should be halved and cut into thick slices.

Light fruit cake

This light alternative to the rich fruit cake is perfect for spring or summer time. I used this recipe for our wedding cake and I also use it for our Easter simnel cake at my cafe-pâtisserie Cake Boy. The raisins and sultanas can be soaked overnight in brandy or rum for a boozy cake.

Serves 6
Preparation time: 20 minutes
Cooking time: 2¼ hours

150g (5oz) unsalted butter, softened
  plus extra for greasing
150g (5oz) golden caster sugar
2 eggs
2 tsp orange-blossom water
finely grated zest and juice of 1 orange
  and 1 lemon
175g (6oz) plain flour
100g (3½oz) glacé cherries
100g (3½oz) chopped mixed peel
100g (3½oz) raisins
100g (3½oz) golden sultanas
2 tbsp apricot jam, sieved

Preheat the oven to 170°C (fan 150°C)/325°F/gas mark 3. Grease a deep 15cm (6in) cake tin with extra butter, and double-line the base and sides with baking paper.

Cream the butter and sugar together in a large bowl using an electric hand whisk until fluffy and light. Beat in the eggs gradually. In a small bowl, mix the orange-blossom water with the zest and juice of the orange and lemon. Sift the flour, add all the dried fruit, then fold into the creamed mixture, using a large metal spoon, followed by the juice and zest mix.

Spoon the mixture into the prepared tin and bake in the preheated oven for 30 minutes. Turn the oven down to 150°C (fan 130°C)/300°F/gas mark 2 and bake for another 1¾ hours until the cake is risen, golden and a skewer inserted in the centre comes out clean. Leave to cool for 15 minutes before removing from the tin, peeling off the paper and transferring to a wire rack to cool completely.

I like to decorate my cake with beautiful large pieces of glacé fruits. You can get these from fine food halls or delicatessens. I glaze the cake first with some apricot jam warmed through in a small pan, then arrange the fruits and glaze again to give that professional look.

Tip

The dried fruits should not sink to the bottom of your cake with this recipe, because the mixture is nice and dense. But if you want to take extra precautions, rolling the fruits in plain flour to lightly coat them will prevent them from sinking.

Beetroot and hazelnut cake

This simple cake has a very earthy taste as well a lovely colour. I wear disposable gloves when grating the beetroot, as my fingers get very stained. As well as being a great source of fibre, this cake is full of good vitamins – and beetroot is allegedly an aphrodisiac too.

Serves 6–8
Preparation time: 25 minutes
Cooking time: 30 minutes

200ml (7fl oz) vegetable oil, plus
    extra for greasing
250g (9oz) golden caster sugar
3 eggs
200g (7oz) plain flour
1 tsp baking powder
2 tsp ground mixed spice
3 tsp milk
150g (5oz) raw beetroot, peeled
    and grated (prepared weight)
100g (3½oz) walnut halves, toasted and
    chopped, plus extra to decorate
100g (3½oz) shelled hazelnuts, toasted
    and chopped, plus extra to decorate
4 tbsp apricot jam, sieved

Preheat the oven to 200°C (fan 180°C)/400°F/gas mark 6. Grease a 900g (2lb) loaf tin with extra oil, then base-line with baking paper.

Pour the oil and the sugar into a bowl and whisk until smooth. Add the eggs and continue mixing until you have a smooth, glossy mixture. Sift in the flour, baking powder and mixed spice and fold it in until well combined, then add the milk and grated beetroot. Mix to incorporate, then finally add the walnuts and hazelnuts.

Pour the mixture into the prepared loaf tin and bake in the preheated oven for 30 minutes or until a skewer inserted in the centre comes out clean.

Cool on a wire rack. Remove the cake from the tin, peel off the paper and place on a serving plate. Heat the apricot jam in a small pan and glaze the cake with it, then sprinkle the top with the extra chopped nuts.

1

2

5

6

Upside-down berry sponge

This upside-down berry sponge is very versatile. You can use any fruits you have left over or that are becoming overripe. The berry version is perfect for the summer, but an alternative with apple and cinnamon served warm would be a perfect winter-warmer. This is best eaten on the day it's made as the juice from the fruits start to run through the light sponge and make it soggy.

Serves 8
Preparation time: 20 minutes
Cooking time: 1 hour

200g (7oz) unsalted butter softened,
    plus extra for greasing
200g (7oz) golden caster sugar
5 eggs
200g (7oz) self-raising flour
300–400g (11–14oz) ripe fresh mixed
    berries (raspberries, strawberries,
    blueberries, etc)
50g (2oz) golden syrup

Preheat the oven to 180°C (fan 160°C)/350°F/gas mark 4. Grease a shallow 22cm (8½in) springform cake tin with extra butter, and then line with baking paper.

Cream the butter and sugar together in a large bowl, using an electric hand whisk at medium-high speed, until light and fluffy. Beat in the eggs, one by one, until well combined. Sift in the flour, then fold it in with a large metal spoon.

Place the berries in the base of the prepared tin. Pour in the golden syrup, then spoon the cake mixture on top. Bake in the preheated oven for 1 hour or until the cake is cooked through. Cool the cake in the tin, then remove the sides of the tin and the paper before serving.

Alternatives

Spiced pear: poach some peeled pear halves in a light syrup flavoured with gin and a few juniper berries. Replace the golden syrup with some light caramel syrup.

Fresh plum: roast the fresh plums, cut in half, in a medium oven (180°C (fan 160°C)/350°F/gas mark 4) with some light brown sugar and some mixed spices. Roast for about 15 minutes or until the fruit is soft and sweet. Get rid of the excess juice and follow the recipe above, replacing the berries with the plums, and omitting the golden syrup.

Tip

Fruits must be just ripe. Never bake with fully overripe fruits, as they will be too mushy.

Flour-free orange and lavender cake

This is one of the most popular recipes we do during our 'French country baking day' at my cafe-pâtisserie Cake Boy. It is inspired by the South of France, and it happens to be gluten-free. If you are not sure about the lavender, you can omit it. You can also change the ingredients to match the seasons; for example, replace the lavender with sun-dried cranberries to make it more Christmassy. The rich, spicy syrup works very well too.

Serves 6
Preparation time: 30 minutes
Cooking time: 1 hour

For the sponge
400ml (14fl oz) sunflower oil, plus extra
   for greasing
350g (12oz) ground almonds
300g (11oz) caster sugar
3 tsp baking powder
8 eggs
finely grated zest of 1 lemon
finely grated zest of 2 oranges,
   ideally Seville
2 tsp dried lavender

For the syrup
juice of the zested lemon and
   oranges above
100g (3½oz) caster sugar
a few cloves
2 tsp ground cinnamon

Preheat the oven to 180°C (fan 160°C)/350°F/gas mark 4. Grease a 20cm (8in) cake tin with extra oil, then base-line with baking paper.

In a mixing bowl, combine the ground almonds, caster sugar and baking powder, mixing together well. Break in the eggs and add the oil, mixing gently together.

Using a fine grater, grate the zest from the lemon and oranges into the mixture then add the dried lavender and mix together.

Turn the cake mixture into the prepared tin, and bake in the preheated oven for an hour. Cover the top of the cake with a piece of foil after about 20 minutes.

Meanwhile, make the syrup. Squeeze the juice from the zested lemon and oranges into a small pan. Add the sugar and spices, and mix together well. Bring to the boil, then reduce the heat and simmer for 3 minutes.

Leave to cool in the tin for 10–15 minutes then turn out onto a serving plate and remove the paper. Pierce the top of the cake several times with a skewer or small, sharp knife. Using a tablespoon, spoon the syrup over the cake, allowing it to soak in.

Tip

If you prefer a cake with a slightly less dense texture, substitute 50 per cent of the ground almonds for finely ground polenta or semolina.

Flour-free chocolate sponge cake

You don't have to have an allergy to be able to enjoy this gooey, rich chocolate cake. It's best served warm straight from the oven with crème fraîche.

Serves 8

Preparation time: 15 minutes

Cooking time: 30 minutes

125g (4½oz) unsalted butter, plus extra
    for greasing

85g (3oz) pure cocoa powder, plus extra
    for dusting

125g (4½oz) good-quality dark chocolate,
    broken into pieces

150g (5oz) golden caster sugar

3 eggs

1 tsp vanilla extract

Preheat the oven to 170°C (fan 150°C)/325°F/gas mark 3. Grease a 20cm (8in) cake tin with extra butter, and dust lightly with some extra cocoa powder.

Place the chocolate and butter in a large heatproof bowl and set the bowl over a pan that is half-filled with gently simmering water. The base of the bowl must not touch the water. Leave to melt, stirring occasionally. Meanwhile, whisk together the sugar, eggs, vanilla extract and the cocoa powder, using an electric hand whisk at medium-high speed, until you create a ribbon effect (see page 18) Remove the chocolate bowl from the heat and stir the egg and sugar mixture into it.

Pour the mixture into the prepared tin and bake in the preheated oven for 30 minutes.

Leave it to cool in the tin for 10–15 minutes, then turn out on to a wire rack to cool down. Or, do like me, and serve it straightaway with crème fraîche.

Tip

Gluten-free flour has come a long way in recent years, and you can substitute it for the flour in any of the cakes in this book if you prefer.

Flour-free almond sponge cake

I personally haven't got any allergies, but more and more people are requesting gluten-free cakes. Even though gluten-free flours are getting better, the yummy alternative is to use ground almonds to bind the recipe, which is what makes this cake so moist and rich.

Serves 6
Preparation time: 15 minutes
Cooking time: 30–45 minutes

100g (3½oz) unsalted butter, melted, plus
    extra for greasing
200g (7oz) golden caster sugar
4 large eggs
200g (7oz) ground almonds
1 tsp almond essence
2 tbsp apricot jam, sieved

Preheat the oven to 180°C (fan 160°C)/350°F/gas mark 4. Grease a 20cm (8in) sponge tin with extra butter, and line with baking paper.

In a large bowl, beat the sugar and eggs together, using an electric hand whisk at medium-high speed, until they double in volume. Whisk in the melted butter and then the ground almonds and the almond essence.

Spoon the mixture into the lined sponge tin, and bake in the preheated oven for 30–45 minutes until the top of the cake is golden brown and the cake is shrinking away from the side of the tin. Allow to stand for 10 minutes before turning out on to a wire rack and removing the paper. Allow to cool.

To decorate, simply heat the apricot jam in a small pan then spread it lightly on top of the cake. You can add some fresh berries or dried fruits and nuts.

This cake is best eaten after a couple of days – and keep it in a cake tin, not in the fridge.

Tarts

Tarts

The tart is a kind of open pie, usually made with sweet shortcrust or puff pastry as a base. Tarts are very versatile. A pastry tart base or case can be fully baked before being filled with cream or custard and fruits and eaten cold; it can be baked from raw with a filling such as a rich almond cream and fruits; or it can be blind-baked first, then filled with a liquid mix as for a lemon or pecan tart.

Many people worry about making pastry. OK, making fresh puff pastry is not easy, and takes time (and patience), but there is no excuse for not attempting sweet shortcrust and choux. The recipes on pages 214–17 (even the puff pastry one!) are simple to follow, and when you've succeeded, you will have to acknowledge that, in taste and texture, there is no comparison between home-made and shop-bought.

The pastry is the key to a good tart. There are a few rules, and I give some tips throughout the recipes. But in short, don't over-mix your pastry; don't use too much flour when rolling; don't stretch the pastry too much (or it will shrink back in the baking); and give your pastry plenty of time to rest when you have finished making it and after you have shaped it.

You can make shortcrust pastry in the food processor, although hand-made tends to be lighter. It is important that, when rolling out, the pastry is warm enough to be pliable, but not so warm as to be dripping fat. For a tart, you want the pastry to be as thick as a £1 coin.

The other important thing in tart-making is baking the pastry, which must be perfectly cooked and crisp. I find I get great results by putting my tart tins on the oven rack instead of on a tray, so that direct heat reaches the base of the tart case pastry.

Tarte bourguignonne

This is a take on the classic tarte Bourdaloue (poached pears cooked in almond cream). The combination of the red wine, spices, pears and the rich chocolate almond cream make this very wintery dessert perfect.

Serves 8

Preparation time: 1 day in advance for
  pears, + 20 minutes, + chilling
Cooking time: 30–40 minutes

unsalted butter, for greasing
plain flour, for dusting
300g (11oz) sweet shortcrust pastry
  (see page 216) or 1 x 375g pack ready-
  rolled sweet shortcrust pastry, chilled
2 tbsp apricot jam, sieved
icing sugar, to decorate

For the poached pears

250g (9oz) caster sugar
200ml (7fl oz) red wine
100ml (3½fl oz) water
2 cinnamon sticks
1 vanilla pod, split
4 large ripe pears (ideally Williams)

For the almond cream

125g (4½oz) ground almonds
125g (4½oz) caster sugar
100g (3½oz) pure cocoa powder
125g (4½oz) unsalted butter, softened
3 eggs

Poach the pears the day before you wish to make the tart. Place the caster sugar, wine, water, cinnamon and vanilla pod in a large saucepan and heat until the sugar has dissolved, making a syrup.

Peel the pears and core them, leaving them whole, and add them to the syrup. (I like to keep the stalks on the pears for a more rustic effect.) Poach the pears for 10 minutes. Set the pears aside to cool in the syrup. Once cool, chill the pears, still in the syrup, overnight in the fridge.

When ready to cook, preheat the oven to 180°C (fan 160°C)/350°F/ gas mark 4. Grease a 22cm (8½in) loose-bottomed flan tin with extra butter.

On a lightly floured work surface, roll out the chilled pastry finely, at least 5cm (2in) larger in diameter than the flan tin. Line the tin with the pastry and chill for 30 minutes.

For the almond cream, mix together the ground almonds, caster sugar and cocoa powder. Add the butter and cream together, using an electric hand whisk (or a wooden spoon) until thoroughly mixed. Beat in the eggs, one by one, and keep beating until smooth.

Fill the pastry case with the almond cream. Halve the poached pears, keeping the stalks intact and slice across horizontally, but without cutting all the way through, at about 3mm (⅛in) intervals to create a fan effect. Lay the pear slices with the fan-effect side up.

Bake the tart in the preheated oven for 30–40 minutes until the filling is set and the pastry pale gold. Gently heat the apricot jam in a small pan. Brush the freshly baked pear tart with the jam to glaze it. Dust the edge of the tart with icing sugar just before serving.

I always serve this tart warm from the oven with some clotted cream or a rich caramel ice-cream.

Alternative

Apricot, plum or apple: You could replace the cocoa in the almond cream with the same weight of ground almonds, and replace the fruit with halved apricots or plums or sliced apples.

Walnut tarts

This tart is very rich and great served for tea. I like making individual ones using some deep tart tins. Make sure you get some very good-quality walnuts: the French and Italian ones are the best.

Serves 8
Preparation time: 20 minutes, + chilling
Cooking time: 30 minutes

unsalted butter, for greasing
600g (1lb 3oz) sweet shortcrust pastry (see page 216), or 2 x 375g packs ready-rolled sweet shortcrust pastry, chilled
plain flour, for dusting

For the filling
150g (5oz) walnut halves
85g (3oz) caster sugar
50ml (2fl oz) water
200ml (7fl oz) double cream
2 tbsp clear honey
2 egg yolks

Lightly grease eight 10cm (4in) tartlet tins with butter. Roll out the pastry on a lightly floured work surface, and cut into circles at least 5cm (2in) wider in diameter than the tartlet tins. Use to line the tins, and place the tins on a baking sheet. Chill for 30 minutes.

Preheat the oven to 170°C (fan 150°C)/325°F/gas mark 3.

Place the walnut halves in a plastic bag and with a rolling pin break them into large pieces.

To make the caramel, melt the sugar with the water in a saucepan until you achieve a nice blond-coloured caramel. Off the heat, add the cream, honey and walnuts. Mix well and then mix in the egg yolks.

Spoon the walnut cream into the pastry cases. Put the baking sheet and its little walnut tarts into the preheated oven and bake for 30 minutes.

If you like, decorate with some walnut halves, glazed with warm sieved apricot preserve. These tartlets are best served warm.

Tips

When making a caramel it is important to follow these simple rules:
- Never stir the caramel. If the sugar starts to caramelize in one part of the pan before the rest, swirl the pan or push the caramelizing sugar forward.
- Ensure no sugar is on the side of the pan before starting to caramelize; if it is, use a wet pastry brush to remove it.
- The caramel is cooked when there is a slow bubble and it is a lovely brown.
- Caramel goes from brown to burned very quickly, so watch it like a hawk and have a sink of cold water ready to dip the pan into as soon as the caramel is cooked.
- A little crystalization, whilst not ideal, does not mean your caramel is ruined; it just gives a slightly different texture.

Bakewell tart

OK, I know what you are thinking. A Frenchman making a Bakewell tart, what next? As with a lot of traditional recipes, classics such as Bakewell lose their popularity because of the commercial use of bad and cheap ingredients, but when done properly they are delicious.

Serves 8
Preparation time: 55 minutes,
    + cooling overnight
Cooking time: 30 minutes

1x 22cm (8½in) blind-baked sweet
    shortcrust pastry tart case
    (see page 216)

For the strawberry filling
100g (3½oz) preserving sugar
juice of 1 lemon
25ml (1fl oz) water
150g (5oz) good-quality fresh
    strawberries, hulled and halved
freshly ground black pepper (optional)

For the almond cream topping
200g (7oz) caster sugar
200g (7oz) ground almonds
200g (7oz) unsalted butter, softened
2 large eggs
2 drops almond essence

To serve
clotted cream

The day before, make the strawberry filling by bringing the sugar, lemon juice and water to the boil. Add the strawberries and cook for 20 minutes on a low heat, so that they form a purée. Using a pepper mill, add a few turns of black pepper (this will intensify the taste). Leave to cool in a bowl overnight.

When ready to bake, preheat the oven to 180°C (fan 160°C)/350°F/ gas mark 4.

To make the almond cream topping, put the sugar, ground almonds and butter into a bowl. Using an electric hand whisk, or a wooden spoon, beat together until light and fluffy. Add the eggs, one at a time, beating them in well, then stir in the almond essence.

Spread the strawberry filling with a palette knife into the base of the tart case. Cover with the almond cream.

Bake in the preheated oven for 30 minutes until the top is lovely and golden and the pastry cooked.

Serve warm with clotted cream.

Pumpkin and pecan tart

This tart is an American classic, combining two of the country's best-known ingredients, the spicy pumpkin base covered with a pecan nut mixture works very well. I like to toast my pecans before making the mixture, as you get a lovely crunch and flavour.

Serves 8
Preparation time: 20 minutes, + chilling
Cooking time: 45 minutes

unsalted butter, for greasing
plain flour, for dusting
300g (11oz) sweet shortcrust pastry
    (see page 216) or 1 x 375g pack ready-
    rolled sweet shortcrust pastry, chilled

For the filling
75ml (2½fl oz) milk
75ml (2½fl oz) double cream
3 eggs
200g (7oz) puréed pumpkin
90g (3¼oz) golden caster sugar
1 tsp ground cinnamon
½ tsp each of ground ginger, ground
    cloves and ground allspice
1 tsp vanilla extract

For the topping
200g (7oz) shelled toasted pecan nuts,
    chopped
85g (3oz) muscovado sugar
3 tbsp melted unsalted butter

Preheat the oven to 180°C (fan 160°C)/350°F/gas mark 4. Grease a 22cm (8½in) loose-bottomed flan tin with butter.

On a lightly floured work surface, roll out the chilled pastry finely, at least 5cm (2in) larger in diameter than the flan tin. Line the tin with the pastry, and chill for 30 minutes.

Place all the filling ingredients in a blender or food processor and blend for 2 minutes. Pour into the tart shell and bake in the preheated oven for 15 minutes. Reduce the heat to 160°C (fan 140°C)/325°F/gas mark 3, and bake for 30 minutes more, or until a skewer inserted in the centre comes out clean. Remove from the oven and let the tart cool.

For the topping, mix the nuts and sugar together. Stir in the melted butter until the mixture is uniformly moist. Sprinkle this over the tart. Grill until lovely and golden.

Serve warm – my favourite way is with crème fraîche.

Austrian coffee tart with raspberries

This light-as-air tart is based on an Austrian classic. It is like a cross between a tart, a meringue and a macaroon.

Serves 8
Preparation time: 10 minutes
Cooking time: 30 minutes

22cm (8½in) blind-baked sweet
    shortcrust pastry tart case (see
    page 216)
3 punnets fresh raspberries
icing sugar, for dusting

For the filling
250g (9oz) icing sugar
1 tbsp coffee extract
4 egg whites

Preheat the oven to 170°C (fan 150°C)/325°F/gas mark 3.

To make the filling, put the icing sugar, coffee extract and one of the egg whites in a large bowl. Using a wooden spoon at first, and then an electric hand whisk, mix and beat them together until really fluffy.

In a separate bowl, whisk the remaining egg whites to soft peaks. Fold these gently into the coffee mixture, using a large metal spoon.

Pour this into the pastry case, and bake in the preheated oven for 30 minutes. Leave to cool.

To serve, cover the top with the fresh raspberries and dust with a little icing sugar.

Apricot and honey tart

This recipe is my take on a traditional tart called *jalousie*, and I have added a Middle Eastern flair to it. I love the flavours of Middle Eastern cooking and baking. Although they're usually a bit too sweet for my palate, this flaky creation is as light as a feather, and tangy.

Serves 6
Preparation time: about 40 minutes,
    + chilling
Cooking time: 25–30 minutes

plain flour, for dusting
300g (11oz) puff pastry (see page 212),
    or 1 x 375g pack ready-rolled puff
    pastry, chilled
1 large egg yolk, beaten with 1 tbsp milk,
    for egg-wash
⅔ tbsp honey

For the filling

300g (11oz) fresh apricots
85g (3oz) golden caster sugar
1 vanilla pod, split
2 tsp water
150g (5oz) cream cheese
2 tsp ground cinnamon
2 eggs

For the filling, wash the apricots, cut them in half and remove the stones. Place the apricot halves in a heavy-based saucepan with the caster sugar, split vanilla pod and water. Give it a good stir around using your fingers or a wooden spoon. Place the lid on the pan and gently heat until the apricots break down and form a purée, which should take about 30 minutes. Remove the vanilla pod, and leave the mixture to cool down.

In the meantime, prepare the pastry. On a lightly floured surface, roll the pastry out to form two rectangles of about 40 x 12cm (16 x 4½in). Using a sharp knife, and leaving a 2cm (¾ in) border, cut regular slashes on one of the rectangles across its width: they should be around 8cm (3¼in) long roughly, separated by a 2–3cm (¾–1¼in) space. Using a brush, egg-wash the top of both pastry rectangles. Place the unslashed rectangle of pastry on a baking sheet, and chill both rectangles for 30 minutes.

Preheat the oven to 200°C (fan 180°C)/400°F/gas mark 6.

In a small bowl mix the cream cheese with the cinnamon and eggs. Using a palette knife, spread the mixture on to the uncut rectangle of pastry, leaving a small border around the edge. Place the cool apricot mixture on top and then place the slashed rectangle of pastry delicately on top. Using your fingers, press the edges, sealing the filling in well.

Use the rest of the egg-wash to glaze the whole tart. Put the baking sheet and tart into the preheated oven and bake for 25–30 minutes until it has puffed up and turned a lovely golden colour. As the pastry cooks, the slashes on the top will open out and give the traditional look to this classic. Leave to cool slightly and drizzle the honey on top.

1

2

3

4

5

6

Fresh fruit tart

This is the beautiful, fresh fruit tart you see in all the pâtisserie windows in France. The fresher it is when you eat it, the better, as there is nothing worse than a fruit tart with a soggy bottom. The basis of the tart is a wonderful crème pâtissière.

Serves 8
Preparation time: 30 minutes + cooling
Cooking time: 20 minutes

1x 22cm (8½in) blind-baked sweet
  shortcrust pastry tart case
  (see page 216)

For the crème pâtissière (makes
  400ml/14fl oz)
4 egg yolks
100g (3½oz) caster sugar
25g (1oz) cornflour
1 vanilla pod, split
350ml (12fl oz) milk

For the crème pâtissière, in a bowl and using an electric hand whisk on medium speed, whisk the egg yolks with the sugar until fluffy, then stir in the cornflour.

Meanwhile, put the vanilla pod in a saucepan with the milk and bring it slowly just to the boil. Remove the vanilla pod and pour the perfumed milk slowly on to the egg mixture, whisking all the time.

Pour the mixture from the bowl back into the milk pan and stir over a medium-low heat until it comes up to a gentle boil (it must boil for it to thicken.) Continue to cook, stirring all the time, for 2 minutes or until it has thickened. I find it easier to use a small whisk.

Remove from the heat and pour the mixture into a bowl. Cover with clingfilm and allow to cool.

Ways of finishing your tart

Tarte aux fraises: Spread a thin layer of good-quality strawberry preserve over the base of the pastry case. Fill the tart with the crème pâtissiere (give it a whisk to loosen as it will have set) and cover with whole or halved fresh strawberries. Glaze with a hot sieved strawberry preserve. Decorate with a few strawberries dipped in chocolate.

Tarte exotique: Cut a disc of vanilla sponge to fit inside the tart base (1cm/½in thick, see page 16). Splash over some dark rum. Cover with crème pâtissiere. Arrange a selection of prepared exotic fruits: papaya, baby mango, passionfruit, berries, starfruit. Glaze with a hot apricot preserve. Sprinkle over some shredded coconut and fresh nutmeg.

Hot raspberry and basil: Cut a disc of vanilla sponge to fit in the tart base (1cm/½in thick, see page 16). Bring 100g (3½oz) caster sugar and 50ml (2fl oz) water to the boil to make a syrup. Remove from the heat and add a handful of fresh basil leaves. Leave to infuse until cold. Sieve the syrup and, with a pastry brush, use it to soak the sponge base. Spread on the crème pâtissiere and cover with fresh raspberries. Just before serving, place in a hot oven (180°C/fan 160°C/350°F/gas mark 4) for 10–15 minutes.

Tip

Rub a small cube of butter over the surface of the hot cream in the bowl to stop a skin from forming.

Pear tarte tatin

A tarte tatin has to be eaten hot: I bake mine during the main course so that it is ready to be turned over at the table with all the lovely juice flowing out. I highly recommend that you buy a proper tarte tatin pan; it has a very thick base that makes the caramelizing part so much easier.

Serves 6

Preparation time: 35 minutes, + chilling
Cooking time: 25 minutes

225g (8oz) puff pastry (see page 212) or
   1 x 375g pack ready-rolled puff
   pastry, chilled
plain flour, for dusting
50g (2oz) unsalted butter, softened
100g (3½oz) golden caster sugar
2 tbsp Poire William liqueur or
   lemon juice
4–6 ripe pears
1 tsp juniper berries

To serve
crème fraîche or fromage frais

Preheat the oven to 220°C (fan 200°C)/425°F/gas mark 7. Have ready a 24cm (9½in) tarte tatin dish, or ovenproof omelette pan.

Roll out the pastry on a lightly floured surface. Then, using a plate that is slightly larger than your pan, cut out a circle of pastry. Lightly prick with a fork and chill while you prepare the remaining ingredients.

Using your fingers, press the butter on to the base of your pan until it coats it evenly. Sprinkle the sugar over the butter and set aside.

Place the liqueur in a large bowl. If you don't want to use alcohol, add lemon juice instead, which will help prevent the fruit discolouring. Prepare the pears one at a time. Peel, cut into quarters and cut out the cores. Toss in the liqueur or lemon juice.

Place the tarte tatin pan on a medium-high heat. Watch the pan carefully at this stage, moving it around if one area is browning faster than another. As soon as the sugar has caramelized, remove from the heat. Scatter the juniper berries into the caramel.

Take the pears from their juice and tightly pack in a circle in the pan, ensuring that their more attractive rounded sides are pressed lightly into the caramelized sugar. Place on a medium-high heat. The pears will shrink slightly as they cook, so do not be afraid to add another pear half or two. Keep cooking for 10–15 minutes until the pears are a nice dark caramel colour.

Take the pan off the heat and quickly press the pastry circle on to the top of the pears, tucking the edges down the side of the pan, then place in the centre of the preheated oven. Bake for 25 minutes or until the pastry is a beautiful golden colour and well risen. Do not worry if some of the caramelized juices bubble out.

Remove from the oven and leave to sit for 5 minutes. Then take a warm serving plate, press against the pastry and invert the pan, giving a good shake. The tart should slip out, juices and all. Serve with lots of crème fraîche or fromage frais.

Tip

Lift the fruit using a knife to check that it is caramelized right through before adding the pastry. It should take on a dark caramel colour within 10–15 minutes and feel bouncy when pressed.

Rhubarb and apple tarte Normande

This French regional tart is lovely as a dessert, as the fruits are cooked in a rich custard. You can play around with whatever is in season; try greengages, cherries, and so on.

Serves 8
Preparation time: 20 minutes
Cooking time: 40 minutes

1 x 22cm (8½in) blind-baked sweet
    shortcrust pastry tart shell
    (see page 216)
unsalted butter, for greasing
icing sugar, for dusting

For the filling
4 apples (Cox's or Granny Smith)
100g (3½oz) rhubarb stalks
    (preferably red)
35g (1¼oz) unsalted butter
100g (3½oz) caster sugar, plus an extra
    2 tbsp
½ tsp ground cinnamon
100ml (3½fl oz) double cream
2 large eggs
1 tbsp Calvados

Preheat the oven to 180°C (fan 160°C)/350°F/gas mark 4.

To start the filling, peel and core the apples, then cut them into large chunks. Trim the rhubarb minimally, then cut into chunks.

In a frying pan, melt the butter with the 100g (3½oz) sugar and the cinammon, and cook the apple and rhubarb for a few minutes, just enough to give a bit of colour and to soften them slightly. Place the apple and rhubarb in the tart case.

In a bowl, mix the cream with the eggs, then add the extra 2 tbsp caster sugar and the Calvados. Pour over the apple mixture right to the top.

Bake in the preheated oven for 40 minutes until it goes a lovely golden colour. Leave to cool in the tin.

Dust the edge of the tart with icing sugar just before serving.

Apple tart with quince

You will find this pâtissier's classic, the apple tart, everywhere in France. A good friend of my grandmother's used to make hers with some slices of fresh quince between the apple, and she glazed it with quince jelly too.

Serves 6

Preparation time: 40 minutes, + cooling
   and chilling
Cooking time: 35 minutes

unsalted butter, for greasing
300g (11oz) sweet shortcrust pastry
   (see page 216) or 1 x 375g pack ready-
   rolled sweet shortcrust pastry, chilled
plain flour, for dusting
quince jelly or sieved apricot preserve,
   to glaze

For the filling

5 large apples (Cox's or Granny Smith)
1 vanilla pod, split
3 tbsp golden caster sugar
1 tsp vanilla extract
1–2 quince (omit if you can't get hold
   of them)

Preheat the oven to 180°C (fan 160°C)/350°F/gas mark 4. Grease a 22cm (8½in) loose-bottomed flan tin with butter.

To start the apple compote, peel and core two of the apples, then cut them into large segments. Place these in a suitable casserole dish with the split vanilla pod and 2 tbsp of the sugar. Put the lid on, and bake in the preheated oven for 30 minutes. Remove from the oven and leave to cool down.

Meanwhile, roll out the pastry on a lightly floured work surface so that it is at least 5cm (2in) larger in diameter than the flan tin. Line the greased flan tin with the pastry. Chill for 30 minutes.

Preheat the oven to the same temperature as above.

Peel and core the remaining apples and the quince, and cut into thin slices. Spread the cool apple compote on top of the pastry with a spatula, and fan the apple slices around the pastry, alternating with some slices of quince. Sprinkle the remaining sugar lightly over the top.

Bake in the preheated oven for 35 minutes or until the pastry is golden brown and the edges of the fruit slices start to colour.

Leave to cool in the tin for 30 minutes. Heat up some quince jelly or sieved apricot preserve in a small pan and brush this over the top of the fruit to give the tart a nice professional look.

Lemon and passionfruit tart

This recipe is based on the traditional tarte au citron. I've never been keen on the 'lemon curd' type, which I find too rich and sweet, but the addition of the passionfruit gives it a lovely zesty tang, perfect to clean the palate after a rich meal. You can add a few fresh raspberries too before baking. But, remember, this tart's success is all to do with the wobble!

Serves 8
Preparation time: 20 minutes
Cooking time: 25–30 minutes

1 x 22cm (8½in) blind-baked sweet
   shortcrust pastry tart shell
   (see page 216)
2 tbsp apricot preserve, sieved, for glazing
icing sugar, to decorate

For the filling
5 eggs
150g (5oz) golden caster sugar
150ml (5fl oz) double cream
finely grated zest and juice of 2 lemons
2 ripe passionfruit, halved

Preheat the oven to 150ºC (fan 130ºC)/300ºF/gas mark 2.

In a bowl, using an electric hand whisk, beat the eggs and sugar until they look pale and fluffy. Stir in the cream, and then the zest and juice of the lemons. With a teaspoon, scoop out the pulp from the passionfruit shells and add to the cream. (I like the look of the black seeds so I leave them in, but you can sift the pulp if you like.) Pour this mixture into a measuring jug.

Place your blind-baked tart case on a baking tray in the preheated oven, and pull out the oven shelf a bit. Pour from the measuring jug to fill the tart case right to the top with the lemon mixture. Slide the shelf carefully back in, and close the oven door.

Bake the tart for 25–30 minutes until the mixture is set but still WOBBLY! Leave to cool down in the tin.

With a pastry brush, glaze the top with a hot apricot preserve and decorate with a dusting of icing sugar.

Tip

When baking a tart with liquid inside, always put a baking tray **beneath** the tart to avoid any filling dripping out on to the oven.

Warm Belgian chocolate tart

This is a warm dessert for the serious chocolate lover. A great way to vary it is to add a couple of punnets of fresh raspberries to the chocolate mixture.

Serves 8

Preparation time: 40 minutes, + chilling

Cooking time: 35 minutes, + resting

For the pastry

100g (3½oz) plain flour, plus extra
  for dusting

85g (3oz) caster sugar

20g (¾oz) pure cocoa powder

85g (3oz) unsalted butter, at room
  temperature, plus extra for greasing

1 egg

For the filling

150ml (5fl oz) whipping cream

100ml (3½fl oz) milk

1 vanilla pod

250g (9oz) dark chocolate, broken
  into pieces

2 eggs

First, make the pastry. In a mixing bowl, combine the flour, caster sugar and cocoa powder. Using your fingertips, rub the butter into the mixture. Then mix in the egg, again by hand, shaping it into a dough. Cover with clingfilm and chill in the refrigerator for 2 hours. (If necessary, the pastry can be made the day before.)

On a lightly floured work surface, roll out the chilled pastry finely, at least 5cm (2in) larger in diameter than a 20cm (8in) loose-bottomed flan tin. Use a little extra butter to grease the tin. Line the tin with the pastry, and chill for 30 minutes.

Preheat the oven to 180°C (fan 160°C)/350°F/gas mark 4.

Meanwhile, for the filling, whisk together the whipping cream and milk in a mixing bowl using an electric hand whisk until well combined. Transfer to a saucepan and bring to a simmer. Cut a slit lengthways along the vanilla pod and add the pod and its seeds to the cream mixture. Set aside to infuse for 10 minutes.

At the same time, melt the chocolate. In a heatproof bowl suspended over a pan of gently simmering water (the bowl should not touch the water), melt the chocolate, stirring occasionally.

Break the eggs into a mixing bowl. Pass half the infused cream mixture through a sieve on to the eggs, and whisk until well blended. Strain the remaining cream mixture into the egg mixture and whisk again. Fold in the melted chocolate using a large metal spoon.

Pour the chocolate mixture into the pastry case. Bake in the preheated oven for 10 minutes. Reduce the oven temperature to 110°C (fan 90°C)/225°F/gas mark ¼, and continue to bake for a further 25 minutes. Then turn off the oven and leave the tart to rest inside the oven for a further 20 minutes.

Serve with clotted cream or whipped cream flavoured with a dash of brandy.

Pastis Gascon

As well as being delicious, this is a very dramatic dessert to serve: it should be cut at the table and the very brittle pastry just explodes everywhere! I usually like to make the pastry myself, but if you're in a rush, use ready-made filo pastry, as here.

Serves 6

Preparation time: overnight soaking,
    + 15 minutes
Cooking time: 40 minutes

150g (5oz) unsalted butter, melted
1 packet ready-made filo pastry

For the filling

3 large apples (Granny Smiths or Cox's),
    peeled, cored and very finely sliced
150g (5oz) pitted prunes, soaked
    overnight in Cognac
200g (7oz) soft dark brown sugar

To serve

vanilla custard (for home-made, see
    Tip page 196)

Preheat the oven to 180°C (fan 160°C)/350°F/gas mark 4. Place a 22cm (8½in) flan ring on a baking sheet. With a pastry brush, grease the inside of the flan ring and the base of the baking sheet with a little of the melted butter.

Separate out the sheets of filo pastry, covering those you are not using with a damp cloth. Brush some melted butter across one sheet of the filo pastry and cut into large, wide bands. Cover the bottom and sides of the ring, in a criss-cross fashion, leaving some pastry overhanging the edges. Repeat the buttering, cutting and criss-crossing operation three times. You want to create a star-like effect with your bands of filo pastry.

Arrange the apple slices and prunes in the tart. Sprinkle the brown sugar over. Crumple the rest of the buttered pastry all over the top. Bake in the preheated oven for 40 minutes until the pastry is crisp and golden.

Serve immediately with vanilla custard.

Tip

When preparing filo pastry, keep the sheets not being used covered with a damp tea-towel to stop them from drying out.

1

2

3

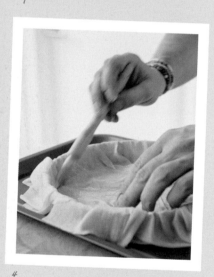

4

5

6

7

8

9

Meringues

Meringues

Meringue is basically a mixture of egg white and sugar, and the combination has been popular for centuries. There are many types of meringue, differing in variations of quantities of ingredients: they can be cooked slowly at a low temperature for a drier and crisper texture; they can be cooked at a high temperature for a marshmallow effect; and they can be cooked (by the inclusion of a sugar syrup) for use as a topping on something like lemon meringue pie.

The secrets to making good meringues are few. One of the most important things is to have all your equipment as clean and dry as possible: any trace of grease will ruin your chances of success. For the same reason, it is essential that you separate the egg yolks and whites carefully: any trace of yolk in the whites will ruin your meringue. I have also found that egg whites at room temperature work better, so pull them out of the fridge well in advance of whipping. And it is also very important that you don't over-whisk the whites, as they will disintegrate.

When adding ingredients such ground nuts or flavourings and so on, I use a large metal spoon to fold them in. This helps ensure that you lose as little air as possible.

Italian meringue

This is a soft cooked meringue used mostly as a topping for lemon pie, in ice-cream or as a base for fruit mousses. The high temperature of the sugar syrup cooks the meringue and pasteurises it. The browning could be done under a grill or, best, with a kitchen blow-torch.

Serves 4–6
Preparation time: 20–30 minutes

300g (11oz) caster sugar
2 tbsp liquid glucose
150g (5oz) egg whites

Combine the sugar, liquid glucose and 4 tbsp water in a thick-based saucepan (preferably copper). Put over a moderate heat and stir until the mixture comes to the boil.

Skim off the surface froth and wash down the crystals at the side of the pan with a clean pastry brush dipped in water. Increase the heat so that the syrup cooks rapidly.

When the syrup temperature reaches 110°C/230°F, whisk the whites in an electric mixer bowl until stiff using the beaters. When the syrup temperature reaches 120°C/248°F, slowly and carefully whisk it into the whisked whites in a thin stream, taking care not to let the syrup run on to the whisk.

Continue beating until the meringue is completely cold, approximately 15 minutes. Use as required in your recipe.

This meringue doesn't keep, so if you have some of the mixture left over, spoon it into a piping bag, pipe on to a baking sheet and slow-dry in a warm (100°C/fan 80°C/212°F/the slowest gas) oven overnight.

Tip

The sugar must not go brown when it is being caramelized; it should be transparent, like a hot sugar syrup. A sugar thermometer is essential for this recipe.

1

2

3

4

Swiss meringue

You can store these meringues in an airtight tin for up to a week. They are often seen piled up in the windows of pâtisseries.

Serves 4–6
Preparation time: 10–15 minutes
Cooking time: 1½–2 hours

4 egg whites
225g (8oz) caster sugar

Preheat the oven to 120°C (fan 100°C)/250°F/gas mark ½. Line two baking sheets with baking paper.

In a large bowl, using an electric hand whisk, whisk the egg whites to soft peaks. Whisk half the sugar, 1 tbsp at a time, into the mixture until stiff. Carefully fold in the rest of the sugar, using a large metal spoon.

Dab a smear of the meringue mixture under each corner of the baking paper to stick it to the baking sheets. Carefully drop spoonfuls of the mixture, spaced well apart, on to the paper.

Bake in the preheated oven for 1½–2 hours until the meringues are dry and lift easily from the paper. Leave to cool at room temperature.

These meringues are delicious sandwiched together with whipped cream. They can also be used to make Eton Mess (see page 92).

Alternatives

Coffee-hazelnut caramel meringues: roast 100g (3½oz) blanched hazelnuts in a medium oven (see page 17) for 10 minutes. In a thick-based saucepan, make a caramel with 100g (3½oz) granulated sugar and 2 tbsp water: heat gently without stirring until the sugar has dissolved, then increase the heat until it is a nice caramel colour. Stir in the nuts, along with a shot of espresso coffee, then pour over an oiled baking tray and leave to cool. Use a rolling pin to break up the hazelnut praline and fold into the meringue mixture just before baking.

Raspberry swirl meringues: I often get asked, how do I get the swirl so pink? Mix 2 teaspoon framboise (raspberry liqueur), 2–3 drops natural raspberry extract or flavouring and a small knife point of red food colouring paste. Mix well and then using a wooden spoon, swirl through the finished meringue mixture just before baking. I like topping my raspberry meringue with freeze-dried raspberries too.

Chocolate swirl meringues: melt 100g (3½oz) dark chocolate (see page 68) and swirl with a wooden spoon through the finished meringue mixture just before baking for a marbled effect.

Caramel meringues: golden caster sugar gives you a caramel taste.

Tip

When whisking egg whites, ensure that your bowl is completely clean and free of any trace of fat. When whisking in the sugar, don't whisk too much, as you can still over-beat the egg whites. Half the sugar is folded in to avoid over-beating. Unrefined sugar will give the meringue a more caramel-like taste and a stickier texture.

1

2

3

4

5

6

Macaroons

These have become so popular! They have been adorning the windows of French pâtisseries for years, but they are now a must for any chic occasion or for gifts. They should be chewy in the middle, and although they don't last for more than three days, they freeze well.

Makes 28 double macaroons

Preparation time: 40 minutes, + resting and cooling

Cooking time: 12–15 minutes

100g (3½oz) ground almonds
100g (3½oz) icing sugar
90g (3¼oz) egg whites (from 3 large eggs)
100g (3½oz) caster sugar

Chocolate macaroons

15g (½oz) pure cocoa powder, sifted

For the filling

dark chocolate ganache

Lemon macaroons

2 drops lemon essence
2 drops yellow food colouring

For the filling

lemon curd (for home-made see Tip page 138)

Rose macaroons

2 drops rose essence
2 drops pink food colouring

For the filling

rose petal preserve

Pistachio macaroons

2 drops pistachio essence
2 drops green food colouring

For the filling

white chocolate ganache

Sift the ground almonds and icing sugar together into a bowl to produce a fine powder.

In a large bowl, using an electric hand whisk, whisk the egg whites at full speed until they start to thicken, then very slowly add the sugar until they form stiff peaks.

Fold the almond mixture into the egg white, along with your chosen flavouring and/or colouring, using a large metal spoon. You will get a stiff, shiny and smooth mixture.

Using a piping bag fitted with a 1.5cm (⁵/₈in) plain tube, pipe 3cm (1¼in) discs on to baking-paper-lined baking sheets. Leave for about 5–10 minutes so that they can dry out a little, while preheating the oven to 150°C (fan 130°C)/300°F/gas mark 2.

Bake in the preheated oven for 12–15 minutes.

As soon as they come out of the oven, lift the baking paper and pour a bit of cold water in between the sheet and the paper. The steam will help to remove the macaroons easily. Cool down on a wire rack.

Once cooled, sandwich the macaroons together with the fillings suggested. Pile together on a plate, and dig in!

 Tip

It is very important to use 90g (3¼oz) egg whites. Egg whites can now be bought in cartons in supermarkets and good food stores, which makes it easier to measure.

1

2

3

4

5

6

7

8

9

Marshmallow strings

I came across these in a fantastic sweet shop in New York. They were selling them out of a big glass jar and cut them with large, gold tailors' scissors.

Serves 6

Preparation time: about 40 minutes,
  + resting

50g (2oz) icing sugar
20g (¼oz) cornflour
250g (9oz) caster sugar
200ml (7fl oz) water
90g (3¼oz) egg whites (from 3 large eggs)
2 tbsp powdered gelatine, dissolved in
  4 tbsp water (see Tip below)
1 vanilla pod, halved

Line a rectangular baking tin about 18 x 28 x 5cm (7 x 11 x 2in, or the longer the better), or a roasting tin, with baking paper, snipping into the corners so that the paper lines the base and sides of the tin.

Mix the icing sugar and cornflour together, then sift half into the tin to dust it generously.

Make a syrup by putting the caster sugar and water into a saucepan, and heating gently, without stirring, until the sugar has dissolved. Increase the heat and boil until it reaches 130°C/266°F, or hard ball on a sugar thermometer.

In the meantime, whisk the egg whites in an electric mixer to achieve stiff peaks.

Pour the hot syrup over the egg whites in a nice small stream. Then whisk in the dissolved gelatine in a thin stream. Scrape the seeds from the vanilla pod into the bowl, and whisk in (or add a different flavouring and colouring – see below).

Scoop the warm mixture into the prepared tray, spread into an even layer and dust with the rest of icing sugar/cornflour mix. Leave to cool and set for at least a couple of hours.

Turn the paper and marshmallow out of the tin, put on a chopping board and peel off the paper. Cut the marshmallow into long strings, using a very sharp knife dipped in hot water. Store in an airtight container, as otherwise they will dry out very quickly.

Alternatives

Use food colouring and flavours to match: raspberry/pink, lilac/lavender, green/pistachio, white/vanilla, and so on.

Tip

Put the water in a medium heatproof bowl, then sprinkle the gelatine over the surface. Tilt the bowl so that all the gelatine powder is absorbed by the water. Leave to stand for 5 minutes, then stand the bowl in a small pan of gently simmering water until the gelatine has dissolved to a clear liquid.

1

2

3

4

5

6

7

8

9

Pavlova

This is based on another type of meringue, originally from Australia, in which the addition of vinegar gives a nice chewy centre. This is the perfect summer dessert with lashings of whipped fresh cream and berries or fruits. I love the rustic look of it, so don't try too hard to make it look perfect. And always do the topping at the last second (not minute!) to stop the meringue going soggy.

Serves 6

Preparation time: about 30 minutes,
    + cooling
Cooking time: 1½ hours

4 egg whites
225g (8oz) golden caster sugar
1 tsp cornflour
1 tsp white wine vinegar
1 vanilla pod, halved

For the topping

300ml (10fl oz) double cream
50g (2oz) vanilla sugar (see Tip below)
seasonal fruits

Preheat the oven to 180°C (fan 160°C)/350°F/gas mark 4. Line a baking sheet with baking paper.

In a bowl, whisk the egg whites with an electric hand whisk until they just form stiff and shiny peaks. Gradually add the sugar, 2 teaspoons at a time, and whisk really well between each addition. Then whisk in the cornflour, vinegar and the seeds scraped from the vanilla pod.

Spoon the mixture on to the baking paper and, using a palette knife, spread into a roughly shaped circle about 20cm (8in) in diameter.

Put the baking sheet into the preheated oven, turn the temperature down to 120°C (fan 100°C)/250°F/gas mark ½ and cook for 1½ hours. Turn the oven off and leave the pavlova inside until completely cool and can be easily peeled off the paper.

Carefully transfer the pavlova on to a serving dish. Don't worry if it cracks.

Whisk the double cream with the vanilla sugar. Just before serving, spoon the cream on top of the pavlova, and top with seasonal fruits.

Alternatives

Tropical pavlova: add 2 tbsp dark rum to the whipped cream and top with slices of fresh mango, pineapple and the pulp scooped out of a halved passionfruit.

Coffee and hazelnut pavlova: before baking, swirl into the pavlova mixture 100g (3½oz) chopped roasted hazelnuts (see Tip page 17) and 2 teaspoons coffee essence, and serve with fresh raspberries.

Chocolate pavlova: swirl 100g (3½oz) melted chocolate (see page 68) into the pavlova mixture before baking. When cooked, top with whipped cream and lots of white, milk and dark chocolate shavings.

Tip

Make vanilla sugar by simply storing a vanilla pod in a container of sugar. The sugar will absorb the vanilla flavour. You can also buy vanilla sugar in some supermarkets.

My Eton mess

This combines my favourite ingredients of meringue, raspberries, mascarpone cheese and cream – and, yes, popping candy. Served in a large glass dish, this dessert looks spectacular and will make everyone's tongues wag!

Serves 6

Preparation time: 20 minutes

2 punnets (350g/12oz) fresh raspberries, plus a few extra to decorate

2 tsp raspberry liqueur (or Grenadine or vodka if you like)

250ml (9fl oz) whipping cream

50g (2oz) vanilla sugar (see Tip page 91)

100g (3½oz) golden caster sugar

250g (9oz) mascarpone cheese

50g (2oz) bought or home-made meringues (see page 78) or meringue nests, broken into pieces

2–3 sachets strawberry popping candy (buy in good sweet shops, or in Cake Boy!)

First of all, make the raspberry coulis or sauce. Place the two punnets raspberries in a saucepan with the liqueur, and cook on a slow heat until the fruits start to soften. Using a fork, mash the mixture up roughly and leave to cool.

In a large bowl, and using an electric hand whisk, whisk the cream with both sugars to nice soft peaks.

In another large bowl, stir the mascarpone around to soften it, then fold in the cream.

Now we are ready to build the mess! In individual glass dishes, in a not too formal way, layer the cream, raspberry coulis and meringue pieces, trying to make it look as attractive as possible. Top with the remaining fresh raspberries and just before serving sprinkle the popping candy on the top. Wait for the astonished reactions to the candy!

Lemon meringue roulade

This meringue has some added ground almonds. The trick is to use a very good-quality lemon curd (home-made is the best). As for the pavlova, fill and roll it at the very last minute to get the maximum lovely crunch; if you do it earlier, the meringue will simply dissolve.

Serves 6
Preparation time: 30 minutes, + cooling
Cooking time: 20 minutes

1 tsp cornflour
1 tsp vanilla extract
1 tsp white wine vinegar
4 egg whites
150g (5oz) caster sugar
75g (2¾oz) ground almonds
40g (1½oz) flaked almonds

For the filling
300g (11oz) lemon curd (for home-made, see Tip page 138)
175ml (6fl oz) whipping cream

To serve
icing sugar, for dusting
seasonal berries

Preheat the oven to 170°C (fan 150°C)/325°F/gas mark 3. Line a Swiss roll tin (it should be 23 x 30cm/9 x 12in when measured across the base) with a sheet of baking paper or a silicone mat.

In a small bowl, blend together the cornflour, vanilla and vinegar to a smooth paste.

Whisk the egg whites in a clean, dry bowl, using an electric hand whisk, until stiff peaks form. Gradually add the sugar, 2 teaspoons at a time, and whisk really well between each addition. Then gently fold the cornflour mixture and ground almonds into the meringue using a large metal spoon.

Spoon the meringue into the prepared cake tin and level the surface with a palette knife. Sprinkle with the flaked almonds.

Bake in the preheated oven for approximately 20 minutes. The meringue should be a pale, golden colour and should feel crisp and dry to the touch. Remove from the oven and leave to cool.

Whip the cream until soft peaks form.

Lay a sheet of baking paper on the work surface and turn the meringue on to it. Peel off the lining paper.

Spread the lemon curd over the meringue. Then spread the cream over the lemon curd. Roll up from one of the long edges, using the paper to help you. The meringue will crack slightly as it is rolled.

Place on a serving dish, and dust generously with icing sugar. Serve cut into thick slices with seasonal berries.

Tip

It is important to make this roulade just before you plan to eat it, as the meringue will start to soften very quickly after filling and rolling.

Baked Alaska

This never loses its charm! Use the best ingredients – plump and juicy fruits and a good-quality ice-cream – and flambé the finished dessert at the table for an impressive party trick!

You will need three rectangular vessels of roughly the same size and shape (loaf tins are good as they can be both baked and frozen).

Serves 8
Preparation time: about 30 minutes,
   + freezing and cooling
Cooking time: 35 minutes

For the ice-cream

1.5 litres (2¾ pints) vanilla ice-cream
125g (4½oz) mixed dried fruits, soaked
   in Grand Marnier

For the sponge

175g (6oz) unsalted butter, softened,
   plus extra for greasing
175g (6oz) caster sugar
3 eggs
finely grated zest and juice of 1 lemon
175g (6oz) self-raising flour, sifted

For the meringue

6 egg whites
400g (14oz) caster sugar

To finish

4 tbsp apricot preserve
25ml (1fl oz) Grand Marnier

Soften your ice-cream (use a mixer with a beater attachment for ease) and add the drained, soaked fruits to it. Pack into one of the loaf tins and re-freeze.

Preheat the oven to 190°C (fan 170°C)/375°F/gas mark 5. Lightly butter one of the remaining loaf tins.

In a bowl, cream together the butter and the sugar, using an electric hand whisk, until light and fluffy. Beat the eggs and add them, a little at a time, combining well after each addition. Once the eggs are thoroughly combined, beat in the lemon zest and lemon juice, then sift on the flour and fold it in, using a large metal spoon.

Turn the batter into your prepared tin, then place in the preheated oven and bake for about 25 minutes or until a skewer inserted into the centre of the cake comes out clean. Allow to cool for 10 minutes in the tin, then turn out on to a wire rack to cool completely.

Once the sponge is completely cold, make your meringue. In a clean bowl, beat the egg whites using an electric hand whisk, gradually adding the sugar until you have a stiff and glossy mixture.

Spread a layer of the meringue on the base of the third loaf tin (not too thick). Cut the sponge in half horizontally and spread the apricot preserve over both the cut ends. Lay one piece of the sponge, jam-side up, over the meringue, then unmould the ice-cream, trim and lay on top. Now place the second piece of sponge, jam-side down, over the ice-cream. Use the remaining meringue to cover the top of the Alaska so that it completely seals the cake, like an igloo! Place the Alaska in the freezer until solid.

Preheat the oven to 220°C (fan 200°C)/425°F/gas mark 7. Remove the Alaska from the freezer and immediately place in the preheated oven. Bake for 8–10 minutes or until the meringue is coloured. You can use a kitchen blow-torch to add a final touch of colour.

In a small saucepan, heat up the Grand Marnier. Carefully light it up and pour over the dessert just before taking it to the table.

Muffins & cupcakes

Muffins & cupcakes

Muffins and cupcakes have become very much part of our home-baking and cake-eating lives. Muffins can be eaten at any time of the day, and are especially good with morning coffee or afternoon tea. I usually add something to the centre of my muffins, often a fruit preserve of some kind, which gives both texture and flavour – and usually surprises the eater as the muffin is bitten into! Cupcakes are much more suited to teatime, but I think they also make an interesting addition to a child's lunch-box.

Try to buy the very best ingredients for your muffins and cupcakes. Your baking trays and paper cases should be chosen carefully too. Metal cases will keep your mufffins and cupcakes moist for much longer than greaseproof ones, but in my house they wouldn't last for long anyway! Make sure you use deep muffin trays and big muffin cases. Always fill the cases right up to the top so that they overflow and give that lovely muffin shape.

When icing your cakes, use a small palette knife or a piping bag. If using the latter, a star tube creates a good effect (see the red velvet cupcakes on page 112); a plain tube is also effective (see the chai tea cupcakes on page 117).

Sugar pearls and sugar flowers make delightful decorations, and sweets such as Smarties or Maltesers, or even whole or sliced fresh fruit, would be good on cakes for children.

Blueberry muffins

Our friends from the other side of the pond make the best muffins and cupcakes. We sell hundreds of these delicious muffins at my cafe-pâtisserie Cake Boy. As well as having the fresh berries, I like to add a compote in the centre, which enhances the flavour and creates a surprise when cutting or biting into.

Makes 12 muffins
Preparation time: 25 minutes
Cooking time: 25 minutes

For the compote
150g (5oz) fresh blueberries
50g (2oz) caster sugar

For the muffins
2 large eggs
200g (7oz) caster sugar
125ml (4fl oz) vegetable oil
½ tsp vanilla extract
250g (9oz) plain flour
½ tsp salt
½ tsp baking powder
250ml (9fl oz) soured cream

First, make the compote. Put the blueberries in a saucepan with the caster sugar and cook gently, stirring from time to time, until the fruits start to burst. Leave to cool.

Preheat the oven to 200°C (fan 180°C)/400°F/gas mark 6. Line a 12-cup muffin tin with muffin papers.

Make the batter for the muffins. In a large bowl, using an electric hand whisk, beat the eggs, gradually adding the sugar while beating. Continue beating while slowly pouring in the oil. Stir in the vanilla.

In a separate bowl, sift together the flour, salt and baking powder. Stir into the egg mixture alternately with the soured cream.

Scoop enough batter into the muffin papers to half-fill them. Spoon 1 tbsp of the blueberry compote over each, and then top with the remaining batter.

Bake in the preheated oven for 25 minutes until the thin blade of an inserted knife comes out clean. Leave to cool on a wire rack.

I like serving mine with some blueberry preserve spread on top – a perfect breakfast or brunch treat.

Peach Melba muffins

These are more of a summery alfresco afternoon type of muffin, and they could almost be served as a dessert, they are so fresh and light.

Makes 12 muffins

Preparation time: 45 minutes, + cooling
Cooking time: 25 minutes

For the peach compote

2 large ripe peaches
100g (3½oz) caster sugar
100ml (3½fl oz) water
½ vanilla pod, split

For the muffins

2 large eggs
200g (7oz) caster sugar
125ml (4fl oz) vegetable oil
½ tsp vanilla extract
250g (9oz) plain flour
½ tsp salt
½ tsp baking powder
250ml (9fl oz) soured cream
1 x 125g (4½oz) punnet fresh raspberries,
   plus a few extra to decorate
125ml (4fl oz) very thick double or
   clotted cream
finely grated zest of 1 lemon
icing sugar, for dusting

First, poach the peaches for the compote. Bring a small saucepan filled with water to the boil. Add the peaches and blanch in the simmering water for 30 seconds. Remove the fruits with a draining spoon, and then with a sharp knife, peel the skin off.

Drain the water from the saucepan, then add the sugar, water and vanilla pod to the saucepan. Make a sugar syrup by bringing this to the boil. Add the peaches and simmer gently for 15–20 minutes. Leave to cool in the syrup. When cool, cut in half, remove the stones and chop the flesh into tiny cubes. Take the vanilla pods out of the syrup, then stir the peach flesh back into the syrup.

Preheat the oven to 200°C (fan 180°C)/400°F/gas mark 6. Line a 12-cup muffin tin with muffin papers.

Make the batter for the muffins next. In a large bowl, using an electric hand whisk, beat the eggs, gradually adding the caster sugar while beating. Continue beating while slowly pouring in the oil. Stir in the vanilla extract.

In a separate bowl, sift together the flour, salt and baking powder. Stir into the egg mixture alternately with the soured cream.

Scoop enough batter into the muffin papers to half-fill them. Drain the syrup from the peach compote, then spoon 1 tbsp of the compote over each and then top with the remaining batter.

Bake in the preheated oven for 25 minutes until the thin blade of a knife inserted comes out clean. Leave to cool on a wire rack.

For the topping, mash the fresh raspberries with a fork roughly. With a small palette knife, spread some cream on top of each muffin, spoon some of the raspberry mash on top, then add a few whole raspberries, if liked. Sprinkle with lemon zest and dust with icing sugar.

Lemon, yoghurt and poppy seed muffins

These zesty muffins will give you a buzz at breakfast! They are light little cakes and the perfect way to kick-start the day.

Makes 12 muffins

Preparation time: 10 minutes

Cooking time: 20 minutes

160g (5½oz) unsalted butter, softened

100g (3½oz) caster sugar

2 eggs

200g (7oz) plain yoghurt

2 tsp lemon juice

½ tsp lemon oil

finely grated zest of 1 lemon

200g (7oz) plain flour

1 tsp baking powder

2 tsp poppy seeds

1 jar good-quality lemon curd or, even
   better, a home-made one (see Tip
   page 138)

Preheat the oven to 180°C (fan 160°C)/350°F/gas mark 4. Line a 12-cup muffin tin with muffin papers.

Cream the butter and sugar together in a bowl using an electric hand whisk, until light and fluffy. Still beating, add the eggs, one at a time. Then stir in the plain yoghurt, lemon juice, lemon oil and lemon zest.

Sift the flour and baking powder together on to the mixture, and stir in with the poppy seeds until just blended, using a large metal spoon.

Scoop enough batter into the paper cups up to half fill them. Spoon in 2 teaspoons lemon curd and top with more batter, this time to the rim of the cups.

Bake in the preheated oven for about 20 minutes. Leave to cool on a wire rack.

Tip

If you are not keen on poppy seeds you can leave them out and make a lemon drizzle instead. Mix 50ml (2fl oz) water with 200g (7oz) icing sugar and the finely grated zest and juice of 1 lemon. Simply drizzle all over the tops of the muffins when they are still warm.

Lemon meringue cupcakes

These cuties are a mixture between a lemon sponge cake and a lemon meringue pie.

Makes 12 cupcakes

Preparation time: 20 minutes

Cooking time: 15–20 minutes

For the cupcakes

100g (3½oz) unsalted butter, softened

100g (3½oz) caster sugar

1 vanilla pod, split

2 eggs

100g (3½oz) self-raising flour, sifted

finely grated zest of 1 lemon

75g (2¾oz) ready-made or home-made
   lemon curd (see Tip page 138)

For the meringue

2 egg whites

100g (3½oz) caster sugar

Preheat the oven to 180°C (fan 160°C)/350°F/gas mark 4. Line a 12-cup muffin tin with cupcake papers.

Cream the butter, sugar and seeds from the vanilla pod together in a large mixing bowl, using an electric hand whisk, until pale, fluffy and well combined.

Crack in the eggs, one at a time, and beat until both are fully incorporated into the mixture. Fold in the sifted flour and lemon zest until well combined.

Spoon the cupcake batter into the cupcake papers. Add 1 tsp lemon curd to the top of each cupcake.

Bake the cupcakes in the preheated oven for 15–20 minutes, or until they are pale golden-brown and spring back when pressed lightly in the centre.

Meanwhile, for the meringue, whisk the egg whites until soft peaks form when the whisk is removed. Gradually add the sugar, whisking continuously, until stiff peaks form when the whisk is removed. The mixture should be thick and glossy.

When the cakes are cooked, turn off the oven and preheat the grill to its highest setting.

Spoon the meringue into a piping bag with a small plain tube and pipe in a spiral on top of each cupcake. Place the cupcakes under the hot grill for 2 minutes to colour (or you can use a kitchen blow-torch to toast the meringue).

Tip

For mess-free filling of the piping bag, put the bag into a tall glass or measuring jug and fold the top over the edges. Fill the bag (don't over-fill it) before removing it from the glass to use.

Toffee and apple sauce muffins

These have to be my favourite of all the muffins we make at the pâtisserie. The combination of the toffee, apple and rich cinnamon is just pure delight!

Makes 12 large muffins
Preparation time: 25 minutes + cooling
Cooking time: 20–25 minutes.

For the apple sauce
300g (11oz) Bramley apples (about
    1 large apple)
100g (3½oz) soft light brown sugar
1 tsp ground cinnamon
2 tsp Calvados

For the muffins
275g (9½oz) plain flour
100g (3½oz) caster sugar
1 tbsp baking powder
75g (2¾oz) unsalted butter, softened
2 large eggs
125ml (4fl oz) full-fat milk
100g (3½oz) home-made or bought fudge,
    chopped into small chunks
2 tbsp cinnamon sugar (2 tbsp soft light
    brown sugar mixed with ¼ tsp
    ground cinnamon)
icing sugar, for dusting

To make the apple sauce, peel and core the apples and cut into small cubes. Place the diced apple in a saucepan with the sugar, cinnamon, Calvados and 1 teaspoon water. Cook over a low heat until the apples are tender but not mushy. Leave to cool.

Preheat the oven to 200°C (fan 180°C)/400°F/gas mark 6. Line a 12-cup muffin tin with muffin papers.

Sift the flour, sugar and baking powder into a large mixing bowl.

Beat the butter and eggs together, then add the milk. Stir this mixture into the flour mixture along with the fudge, until just incorporated. Don't over-stir; it's fine if the mixture is a little lumpy.

Spoon half the mixture into the muffin cases, then spoon over two-thirds of the apple sauce. (Ensure that the sauce is the same consistency as the batter so that it doesn't sink into the cakes.) Cover with the remaining muffin batter. With a small spoon make a swirl of apple sauce in the top and dust with lots of cinnamon sugar.

Bake in the preheated oven for 20–25 minutes. Cool on a wire rack.

Serve dusted with icing sugar. They are also fantastic warm with the steamy apple sauce centre and melting fudge!

Roasted banana muffins

This is a serious banana muffin! No banana flavouring or extract, just the delicious flavour of ripe oven-roasted banana. The cheeky drop of dark rum makes these little cakes even more indulgent and naughty!

Makes 12 muffins
Preparation time: 40 minutes
Cooking time: 20 minutes

For the muffins
2 large, ripe bananas
50g (2oz) soft dark brown sugar
1 tsp vanilla extract
1 tsp ground cinnamon
2 tsp dark rum (optional, but sooo nice!)
85g (3oz) unsalted butter
2 eggs
125ml (4fl oz) milk
250g (9oz) self-raising flour
1½ tsp baking powder
125g (4½oz) caster sugar

For the topping
dried banana chips

Preheat the oven to 180°C (fan 160°C)/350°F/gas mark 4. Line a 12-cup muffin tin with cupcake papers.

First, roast the bananas. Peel them, then place them on a large sheet of foil on a baking sheet. Sprinkle them with the dark sugar, vanilla extract, cinnamon and rum (if using). Wrap up in a loose, but secure parcel (*en papillote*), and cook in the preheated oven for 15–20 minutes. Leave to cool.

Melt the butter and allow to cool. In a bowl, mash the roasted bananas well. With a fork, beat the eggs, melted butter and milk in a second bowl. Add the mashed banana and stir through.

Sift the flour, baking powder and caster sugar into a large bowl. Make a well in the centre and add the egg and banana mixture, stirring roughly with a fork (don't over-mix) until it is a lumpy paste.

Spoon the mixture into the paper cups to the rims. Top each one with some banana chips. Bake in the preheated oven for 20 minutes. Rest the muffins on a wire rack to cool down.

I like serving mine warm with some plain Greek yoghurt with a swirl of clear honey and chopped skinned pistachios.

Wholemeal courgette and seed muffins

For the health conscious, or if you want to trick the kids into eating their fibre, this is a perfectly delicious treat.

Makes 12 muffins
Preparation time: 15 minutes
Cooking time: 25 minutes

For the muffins
225g (8oz) wholemeal plain flour
1½ tbsp baking powder
½ tsp salt
1 tsp ground cinnamon
175ml (6fl oz) milk
2 eggs, lightly beaten
4 tbsp vegetable oil
4 tbsp clear honey
125g (4½oz) grated courgette

For the topping
½ tsp each of pumpkin seeds, sunflower
    seeds and rolled oats, mixed together

Preheat the oven to 180°C (fan 160°C)/350°F/gas mark 4. Line a 12-cup muffin tin with muffin papers.

Sift the wholemeal flour, baking powder, salt and cinnamon into a bowl and mix thoroughly. The bran from the wholemeal flour will collect in the sieve, but just tip this back into your mixture.

Mix the milk, eggs, oil, honey and grated courgette together in another bowl. Pour into the dry ingredients and stir to mix thoroughly. This batter is heavier than the usual muffin batter.

Fill the muffin cups to the rim with batter, and top with the mixture of seeds and oats. Bake in the preheated oven for 25 minutes until risen and golden and an inserted skewer comes out clean. Leave to cool on a wire rack.

Red velvet cupcakes

This is my American friend Laury's recipe, which was passed on to her by a relative. Unlike most cupcake recipes, there's not a hint of food colouring in this mixture. Instead, the rich colour is obtained from the reaction of the bicarbonate of soda with the vinegar.

Makes 24 cupcakes
Preparation time: 30 minutes
Cooking time: 20 minutes

For the cupcakes
75g (2¾oz) pure cocoa powder
1½ tsp vanilla extract
125g (4½oz) unsalted butter, softened
250g (9oz) caster sugar
4 egg yolks
240ml (8½fl oz) buttermilk
1 tsp fine salt
325g (11½oz) plain flour, sifted
1 tsp bicarbonate of soda
1 tsp white wine vinegar

For the frosting
240ml (8½fl oz) milk
3 tbsp plain flour
a pinch of fine salt
225g (8oz) of either dark chocolate
    (62% cocoa solids) or white chocolate,
    broken into pieces
200g (7oz) unsalted butter, softened
300g (11oz) icing sugar
2 tbsp pure cocoa powder (omit if
    making white chocolate frosting)
1 tsp vanilla extract (omit if making
    white chocolate frosting)

Preheat the oven to 180°C (fan 160°C)/350°F/gas mark 4. Line two 12-cup muffin tins with cupcake papers.

Sift the cocoa and mix with the vanilla in a small bowl. Set aside.

Beat the butter and sugar together in a large bowl, using an electric hand mixer set on medium-high speed, or a free-standing mixer. Once the butter and sugar mixture is pale, light and fluffy, add the egg yolks, one at a time, and beat until everything is combined. Add the cocoa mixture and beat well for another minute to combine.

Stir the buttermilk and salt together and add it to the butter and sugar mixture, a third at a time, alternating with the flour. Mix the bicarbonate of soda with the vinegar and blend into the batter. Then, with your mixer on high, beat everything together on a high speed for about 5 minutes, until you have a smooth, glossy batter.

Fill each cupcake case to three-quarters full. Bake for 18–20 minutes or until a skewer inserted in the cupcake centre comes out clean.

Cool in the tins on a wire rack for 10 minutes. Remove the cakes and cool completely before frosting.

For the frosting, whisk the milk, flour and salt in a small saucepan over a medium heat until the mixture thickens and begins to bubble, about 1–2 minutes. Transfer to a small bowl and allow to cool.

Melt dark or white chocolate. Set aside to cool.

Beat the butter, sugar and cocoa (if using) together until fluffy. Add to the cooled chocolate followed by the milk mixture and vanilla extract (if using). Beat together until smooth, then spoon into a piping bag with a small plain or star tube. Pipe immediately on to the cupcakes.

Tip

It is really important that an electric hand-held or free-standing mixer is used to blend the cupcake batter thoroughly, so that a loose, glossy mixture is achieved.

Double chocolate marshmallow muffins

These are a chocoholic's dream! As much as I hate to admit it, I've been seen placing these muffins when cold in a microwave for a moment or so, and serving them warm with some ice-cream. Divine!

Makes 12 muffins
Preparation time: 10 minutes, + cooling
Cooking time: 20 minutes

For the muffins
2 large eggs
175ml (6fl oz) vegetable oil
300ml (10fl oz) milk
500g (1lb 2oz) self-raising flour
a good pinch of salt
2 tsp baking powder
4 tbsp pure cocoa powder
250g (9oz) caster sugar
4 tbsp dark chocolate nuggets/chips
150g (5oz) mini marshmallows

For the decoration
1 jar Marshmallow Fluff topping (buy in larger supermarkets and specialist food halls)
sweetened cocoa powder, for dusting
icing sugar, for dusting

Preheat the oven to 200°C (fan 180°C)/400°F/gas mark 6. Line a 12-cup muffin tin with muffin papers.

Put the eggs and oil into a large jug and mix them together, then mix in the milk.

Next sift the flour, salt, baking powder, cocoa powder and sugar together into a large bowl. Now add the jug of egg mixture to the bowl of dry mixture and mix until it all comes together. Fold in the chocolate nuggets/chips.

Scoop enough batter into the muffin papers to half-fill them. Divide about three-quarters of the mini marshmallows between the centres of the muffins, and then top with the remaining batter.

Bake in the preheated oven for 20 minutes until the thin blade of a knife inserted comes out clean. Leave to cool on a wire rack.

Using a palette knife, smooth the marshmallow topping on top of each muffin. Add the remaining mini marshmallows and dust with sweetened cocoa powder and icing sugar.

Tip

Don't add the Marshmallow Fluff topping until you are ready to serve, as it will start to melt.

Chai tea cupcakes

These original cupcakes have a great flavour. I tried them first in New York with a vanilla base, but I much prefer this chocolate one. Chai is a mixture of tea leaves and spices (cinnamon, fennel, cloves, etc) originally from India. Chai tea mix is available from all good supermarkets.

Makes 12 cupcakes

Preparation time: 15 minutes,
   + cooling and chilling
Cooking time: 15 minutes

For the cupcakes

125g (4½oz) plain flour
25g (1oz) pure cocoa powder, plus extra
   for dusting
25g (1oz) instant chai tea mix
1 tsp baking powder
¼ tsp fine salt
100g (3½oz) unsalted butter, softened
150g (5oz) caster sugar
2 large eggs
½ tsp vanilla extract
80ml (2¾fl oz) milk

For the orange and chai butter-cream frosting

200g (7oz) unsalted butter, softened
50g (2oz) instant chai tea mix
60g (2¼oz) icing sugar, plus extra
   for dusting
finely grated zest of 1 orange

Preheat the oven to 180°C (fan 160°C)/350°F/gas mark 4. Line a 12-cup muffin tin with cupcake papers.

Combine the flour, cocoa, chai mix, baking powder and salt in a bowl, and mix together.

In a large mixing bowl, cream the butter and sugar together, using an electric hand whisk on medium speed. This will take about 3 minutes. Add the eggs one at a time and beat in well. Then stir in the vanilla.

With the whisk on low speed, alternately add the flour mixture and milk to the creamed butter mixture and beat until well combined and smooth.

Fill the cupcake cups with this batter up to three-quarters full. Bake in the preheated oven for about 15 minutes or until risen, and an inserted skewer comes out clean. Let the cupcakes cool completely on a wire rack before frosting.

For the frosting, combine all the ingredients in a bowl and mix with a wooden spoon until smooth. Refrigerate until the cakes have cooled.

Spread or pipe the frosting on top of the cupcakes and, if you like, sprinkle with extra cocoa powder and icing sugar to decorate.

Vanilla cupcakes

This cupcake is the perfect one to make and decorate for parties, birthdays, weddings or seasonal festivities.

Makes 12 cupcakes
Preparation time: 15 minutes, + cooling
Cooking time: 18 minutes

175g (6oz) self-raising flour
150g (5oz) plain flour
125g (4½oz) unsalted butter, softened
250g (9oz) caster sugar
2 large eggs, at room temperature
125ml (4fl oz) milk
½ tsp vanilla extract

Preheat the oven to 180°C (fan 160°C)/350°F/gas mark 4. Line a 12-cup muffin tin with cupcake papers.

In a small bowl, combine the flours and then set aside.

In a large bowl, using an electric hand whisk at medium speed, cream the butter until smooth. Add the sugar gradually and continue beating until fluffy, about 3 minutes. Add the eggs, one at a time, beating well after each addition.

Add the flour in three stages, alternating with the milk and vanilla. With each addition, beat until the ingredients are incorporated, but do not over-beat. Using a rubber spatula, scrape down the batter in the bowl to make sure the ingredients are well blended.

Carefully spoon the batter into the cupcake papers, filling them about three-quarters full. Bake in the preheated oven for 18 minutes.

Cool the cupcakes in the tins for 15 minutes. Remove from the tins and cool completely on a wire rack before icing.

Ice the cupcakes with either vanilla butter-cream (see page 120) or cream cheese frosting (see page 122).

Vanilla butter-cream frosting

This recipe is simple, and doesn't contain eggs. It's really the traditional topping for a cupcake, and ideal if you aren't a fan of cream cheese toppings. It has a beautiful smooth texture, and will add a classic finish to your cakes.

For 12 cupcakes
Preparation time: 10 minutes

250g (9oz) unsalted butter, softened
1 tsp vanilla extract
600g (1lb 5oz) icing sugar
2 tbsp milk

In a large bowl, cream the butter using an electric hand whisk on medium speed. Blend in the sugar, a quarter at a time, beating well after each addition. Beat in the milk and vanilla extract, and continue mixing until light and fluffy.

Keep the frosting covered until ready to decorate the cupcakes. The icing can be coloured by using natural food colouring. I prefer to use a paste colouring instead of liquid, as it doesn't affect the consistency of the frosting.

Using a small palette knife, smooth the frosting over the cupcakes. You can also use the palette knife to create small spikes. Decorate with small sugar beads or sugar flowers, or even sweets such as Smarties or Maltesers.

1

2

3

4

5

6

Cream cheese frosting

This is my favourite cupcake topping, and the one we use in my cafe-pâtisserie Cake Boy. It's rich, creamy and zesty, and adds the finishing touch to a perfect cupcake.

For 12 cupcakes
Preparation time: 15 minutes

50g (2oz) white chocolate, broken
   into pieces
200g (7oz) cream cheese, softened
100g (3½oz) unsalted butter, softened
1 tsp vanilla extract
500g (1lb 2oz) icing sugar

Put the chocolate pieces in a heatproof bowl that fits over a pan of very gently simmering water (the base must not touch the water), and stir until it melts and is smooth. Be careful, as white chocolate is more temperamental than dark. Allow to cool to room temperature.

In a bowl, using a wooden spoon or electric hand whisk, beat together the cream cheese and butter until smooth. Mix in the white chocolate and the vanilla extracts. Gradually beat in the icing sugar until the mixture is fluffy.

Using a small palette knife, smooth the frosting over the cupcakes. You can also use the palette knife to create small spikes. Decorate with small sugar beads or sugar flowers, or even sweets such as Smarties or Maltesers.

You can colour the frosting if you like, and have even more fun decorating your cakes. Use a natural food colouring, preferably a paste.

1

2

3

4

5

6

Tray bakes

Tray bakes

Most tray bakes are the simplest of all sweet bakes. Brownies, for instance, are much quicker to make than a cake, and look just as glamorous. Because of the tray bake's simplicity, it is especially important to use very good-quality ingredients.

If cooking brownies, ensure that they are dense and gooey in the middle, but paler and crisper on the top. If they are not quite ready when you first take them out of the oven, keep checking them. It only takes a matter of minutes in the oven for a perfect brownie to turn into a dry one.

You can choose from a variety of flavourings for brownies: dried fruit like cherries, and nuts such as walnuts, peanuts, hazelnuts or pecans go perfectly with the chocolate.

Kids love tray bakes, and the Malteser cakes and marshmallow squares are really for them. I know they're not really 'bakes', more fridge cakes, but how could I not include these children's favourites?

Blondies with peanut butter

If blondes have more fun, here is the proof! These little cakes have the same texture as a brownie, but use white chocolate and peanut butter for a lighter, sweeter flavour.

Makes 12 blondies
Preparation time: 30 minutes
Cooking time: 40 minutes

100g (3½oz) unsalted butter, softened, plus extra for greasing
150g (5oz) crunchy peanut butter
1 tsp vanilla extract
175g (6oz) caster sugar
1 egg
75g (2¾oz) white chocolate, plus extra to decorate
75g (2¾oz) walnut halves, chopped, plus extra to decorate
125g (4½oz) plain flour
1 tsp baking powder
dark chocolate, melted, to decorate

Preheat the oven to 170°C (fan 150°C)/325°F/gas mark 3. Grease a 20cm (8in) square tin with extra butter, and base-line with baking paper.

In a large bowl, beat the butter and peanut butter together until creamy, using an electric hand whisk at medium speed. Add the vanilla, sugar and the egg, and beat again until light and creamy.

Chop up the white chocolate, and stir in to the mixture along with the chopped walnuts.

Sift the flour and baking powder on to the mixture, and fold in, using a large metal spoon.

Spoon the mixture into the prepared tin and smooth the top. Bake in the middle of the preheated oven for 40 minutes until it has a nice golden crust but is still fudgy in the middle.

Leave to cool in the tin. Decorate with white chocolate chunks and walnut pieces and drizzle over some melted dark chocolate (see Tip below). Cut into squares or triangles.

Tip

Ideally, use a paper cornet to drizzle on melted chocolate. If you don't have one, a metal spoon will suffice, or you can make one by rolling a square of greaseproof paper into a cone and snipping off the tip.

Cream cheese brownies

This takes the best of a rich, traditional brownie, but gives it a twist: the soft cream cheese adds a soft touch as well as a fresh sour-zesty taste.

Makes 12 brownies
Preparation time: 30 minutes
Cooking time: 30 minutes

For the cake
150g (5oz) unsalted butter, plus extra
  for greasing
200g (7oz) dark chocolate, broken
  into pieces
100ml (3½fl oz) freshly made strong
  espresso
250g (9oz) caster sugar
1 tsp vanilla extract
a pinch of salt
3 eggs
100g (3½oz) plain flour

For the marbling mixture
150g (5oz) cream cheese
60g (2¼oz) caster sugar
1 egg, beaten
1 tsp vanilla extract

Preheat the oven to 180°C (fan 160°C)/350°F/gas mark 4. Grease a 20cm (8in) square tin with extra butter, and line it with baking paper.

Melt the butter and the chocolate in a large heatproof bowl over a pan of gently simmering water, stirring occasionally (the bowl should not touch the water). Remove the bowl from the heat and cool slightly.

Stir the sugar, vanilla and salt into the butter-chocolate mixture, then whisk in the eggs, using a wooden spoon or electric hand whisk, and beat until smooth. Stir in the coffee, then sift in the flour and carry on beating until glossy. Set aside.

For the marbling mixture, in a bowl beat the cream cheese until smooth, then stir in the sugar, egg and vanilla.

Spoon the first, dark mixture into the prepared tin, then add the cheese marbling mixture and use a knife to cut through to create a marbled effect. Bake in the preheated oven for 30 minutes. You may need to cover the tin with foil for the last 10 minutes of cooking.

Allow to cool in the tin, then cut into squares.

1

2

5

6

8

3

4

7

9

10

Double chocolate pecan brownies

These lovely, rich, nutty and chewy brownies are an ideal indulgent snack, as well as making the perfect dinner-party dessert. Served with your favourite ice-cream, of course!

Makes 12 brownies
Preparation time: 45 minutes
Cooking time: 25 minutes

185g (6½oz) unsalted butter, plus
    extra for greasing
185g (6½oz) best dark chocolate, broken
    into pieces
85g (3oz) plain flour
40g (1½oz) pure cocoa powder
50g (2oz) white chocolate
50g (2oz) milk chocolate
3 large eggs
275g (9½oz) golden caster sugar
100g (3½oz) pecan halves, chopped

Preheat the oven to 170°C (fan 150°C)/325°F/gas mark 3. Grease a shallow brownie tray or regular square tin (22cm/8½in) with extra butter, and line with baking paper.

Cut the butter into cubes and tip into a medium heatproof bowl along with the dark chocolate pieces. Sit the bowl over a pan of gently simmering water (the base of the bowl must not touch the water) and leave over a low heat until the butter and chocolate have melted, stirring occasionally to mix them. Remove the bowl from the pan and allow to cool a little.

Tip the flour and cocoa powder into a sieve held over a medium bowl.

With a large sharp knife, chop the white and milk chocolate into chunks on a board. (Most supermarkets or delis sell chocolate in buttons, so there is no need for chopping!)

Break the eggs into a large bowl and tip in the sugar. With an electric mixer on maximum speed, whisk the eggs and sugar until they look thick and creamy. You'll know it's ready when the mixture becomes really pale and about double its original volume.

Pour the cooled chocolate mixture over the eggy mousse, then gently fold together with a rubber spatula. Add the sifted flour and cocoa mixture, and gently fold in using a large metal spoon. Finally, stir in the white and milk chocolate chunks and chopped pecans until they're dotted evenly throughout the mixture.

Pour the mixture into the prepared tin. Bake in the preheated oven for 25 minutes. The brownies are cooked when you get a nice cracked and crunchy crust on top, but still with a wet fudgy middle.

Leave the whole thing in the tin until completely cold, then remove, peel away the paper and cut into squares using a sharp knife.

Millionaire shortbread

This is quite simply pure indulgence – crunchy buttery shortbread with a rich caramel middle, and topped with dark chocolate. A real pick-me-up.

Makes 16 biscuits

Preparation time: 30 minutes, + cooling and setting

Cooking time: 20 minutes

For the shortbread

175g (6oz) unsalted butter, cut into small pieces, plus extra for greasing

250g (9oz) plain flour

85g (3oz) caster sugar

For the caramel

100g (3½oz) unsalted butter

100g (3½oz) light muscovado sugar

750g (1lb 10oz) condensed milk

For the topping

200g (7oz) dark or milk chocolate, broken into pieces

Preheat the oven to 180°C (fan 160°C)/350°F/gas mark 4. Lightly grease a 33 x 23cm (13 x 9in) Swiss roll tin with extra butter.

To make the shortbread, mix the flour and caster sugar in a bowl. Rub in the butter until the mixture resembles fine breadcrumbs. Knead the mixture together until it forms a dough, then press into the base of the prepared tin. Prick the shortbread lightly with a fork and bake in the preheated oven for about 20 minutes or until firm to the touch and very lightly browned. Cool in the tin.

To make the caramel, put the butter, sugar and condensed milk into a pan and heat gently until the sugar has dissolved. Bring to the boil, stirring all the time, then reduce the heat and simmer very gently, stirring continuously, for about 5 minutes or until the mixture has thickened slightly. Pour over the shortbread and leave to cool.

For the topping, melt the chocolate slowly and carefully in a heatproof bowl over a pan of hot water (the base of the bowl must not touch the water). Pour over the cold caramel and leave to set.

To serve, cut into squares or bars.

Exotic fruit tray bake

These flapjack-like biscuits will be a hit with the young ones, and make perfect snacks for lunch-boxes or parties. They keep very well in an airtight container. Feel free to be imaginative and replace the fruits with your favourites, or add some nuts. This is a great quick and easy recipe to make with children too.

Makes 12 pieces
Preparation time: 10 minutes
Cooking time: 25 minutes

150g (5oz) unsalted butter, plus extra
   for greasing
75g (2¾oz) soft dark brown sugar
75g (2¾oz) golden syrup
225g (8oz) porridge oats
75g (2¾oz) dried exotic fruit (coconut,
   papaya, pineapple, etc)
a pinch of salt

Preheat the oven to 180°C (fan 160°C)/350°F/gas mark 4. Grease a 24 x 20cm (9½ x 8in) baking tin with extra butter and line, base and sides, with baking paper.

Gently melt the butter, sugar and syrup in a saucepan, but don't let it boil. Stir in the porridge oats, chopped exotic fruits and salt, and mix thoroughly. Press the mixture firmly with the back of a metal spoon into the prepared baking tin.

Bake in the preheated oven for 25 minutes or until golden brown.

Remove from the oven and leave for a few minutes before marking into slices.

Allow to cool a little longer, about 15 minutes, and then, using the edges of the greaseproof, lift the tray bake from the tin and place on a wire rack on the paper. Leave to cool before cutting.

Lemon curd squares

A refreshing and crunchy little treat for both adults' and children's lunch-boxes.

Makes 12 squares
Preparation time: 10 minutes
Cooking time: 40–45 minutes

For the shortbread
175g (6oz) unsalted butter, cut into small
    pieces, plus extra for greasing
200g (7oz) plain flour
85g (3oz) icing sugar, plus extra
    for dusting
1 tsp vanilla extract
icing sugar, for dusting

For the lemon filling
3 eggs
300g (11oz) caster sugar
3 tbsp plain flour
4 tbsp lemon juice

Preheat the oven to 180°C (fan 160°C)/350°F/gas mark 4. Grease a 33 x 23cm (13 x 9in) baking tin with extra butter.

To make the shortbread, mix the flour and icing sugar in a bowl. Rub in the butter until the mixture resembles fine breadcrumbs. Knead the mixture together until it forms a dough, then pat into the base of the prepared tin. Prick the shortbread lightly with a fork, and bake in the preheated oven for 20 minutes until slightly golden.

While the shortbread base is baking, whisk together the eggs, caster sugar, flour and lemon juice until frothy, using an electric hand whisk. Pour this lemon mixture over the hot shortbread.

Return to the preheated oven for an additional 20–25 minutes or until light golden brown. Cool on a wire rack.

Dust the top with icing sugar and cut into squares.

Tip

The lemon curd above, as it is, is not suitable for other recipes in this book that use lemon curd. However, you can make it fit the bill by simply simmering it in a saucepan for 5 minutes to achieve a custard-like texture, whisking all the time to prevent it splitting. Leave to cool completely so that it sets.

Marshmallow bars

A perfect children's party treat. Crisp and chewy, you can even add a touch of fun by using coloured marshmallows to get you in the party mood!

Makes 12 bars

Preparation time: 10 minutes, + cooling and setting

vegetable oil

2 tbsp melted salted butter

200g (7oz) mini marshmallows

1 tsp vanilla extract

600ml (1 pint) Rice Krispies (measure in a measuring jug)

Use a little oil to grease a 23cm (9in) square cake tin.

Melt the butter and 1 tbsp oil together in a large pan over a low heat. Add the marshmallows and stir continuously until they are completely melted. Add the vanilla extract and the Rice Krispies, stirring until well coated.

Press the mixture into the prepared pan and allow to cool and set for about 30 minutes.

Cut into bars or squares.

Tip

As the mixture is very sticky when melted, grease your hand with a bit of oil when pressing the mixture into the tin. This will prevent it sticking to your hands.

Malteser squares

If you are looking for a different way to eat one of our favourite sweets, try this recipe –
I think it's even more moreish than nibbling Maltesers from the bag! Take time to add the
suggested decoration to the top of this delicious tray bake – it makes all the difference.

Makes 20 small squares
Preparation time: 15 minutes, + chilling

100g (3½oz) unsalted butter, plus extra
    for greasing
200g (7oz) milk chocolate, broken into
    pieces
3 tbsp golden syrup
225g (8oz) digestive biscuits, finely
    crushed
225g (8oz) Maltesers

For the decoration
100g (3½oz) Maltesers
50g (2oz) white chocolate, melted (see
    page 122)
50g (2oz) milk chocolate, melted (see
    page 198)

Grease a shallow 20cm (8in) square cake tin with extra butter, and
line, base and sides, with baking paper.

In a medium pan, melt together the butter, milk, chocolate and syrup,
stirring together until smooth. Add the crushed biscuits and stir until
well coated in the chocolate mix. Add the Maltesers and stir together
quickly so that the chocolate covering on the outside of the Maltesers
does not melt.

Tip into the prepared tin, press into an even layer and chill until set.

Lift out of the tin, using the paper, and cut into small squares
to serve.

For a special occasion, before cutting, sprinkle with the chopped
Maltesers, and drizzle with alternate lines of the melted white and
melted milk chocolate (see Tip page 128).

Rocky road fridge cake

Who could resist a slice of this show-stopper? The combination of bright red cherries, pink marshmallows and crunchy biscuit make it a feast for the eyes as well as the taste buds! Ideal for popping in a picnic hamper or handing round to your friends when they come for tea.

Makes 16 squares

Preparation time: 15 minutes, + chilling

100g (3½oz) unsalted butter, plus extra for greasing

200g (7oz) milk chocolate, broken into pieces

200g (7oz) chocolate chip cookies (see page 200), lightly crushed

100g (3½oz) mini marshmallows (the coloured ones are best)

100g (3½oz) red glacé cherries

100g (3½oz) golden sultanas

For the decoration

extra marshmallows, cherries and chocolate chips

35g (1¼oz) dark chocolate, melted (see page 198)

Grease an 18cm (7in) square baking tin with extra butter, and line, base and sides, with baking paper.

Melt the chocolate in a bain-marie (see page 198). Melt the butter and mix into the melted chocolate, then leave to cool for 10 minutes.

Stir the crushed cookies, the mini marshmallows, cherries and sultanas into the cooled chocolate mixture. Transfer to the prepared tin, press down and allow to cool, then chill for at least 2 hours until fully set.

Once set, cover the top with a mixture of marshmallows, cherries and chocolate chips, and drizzle with melted chocolate. When set once more, slice into 16 squares.

Festive
recipes

Festive recipes

I couldn't write a book on home baking without adding a few of my favourite festive recipes. At Christmas my house smells so yummy with all the baking going on, particularly when the long-baked traditional Christmas cake is in the oven. My chocolate and orange Christmas cake is a great alternative, and very tasty.

Back home in France, we celebrate Christmas on Christmas Eve, and when I was a child we would always eat our *bûche de Noël* at midnight, just before 'Père Noël' paid us a visit! Of course we would have the traditional *buche de Noël,* but my chocolate and chestnut one on page 159 is very moreish.

How to decorate your Christmas cake:

The Christmas cake is at the heart of the festive celebrations so it's crucial to get it right. To decorate, knead 450g (1lb) marzipan until soft. Roll out half of it big enough to fit the top of your cake, and the rest in strips to fit around the side. Brush the cake with a warmed apricot glaze then lay the marzipan on top and around the sides and trim as necessary. Cover and leave overnight.

Make the royal icing as on page 219. Spread it all over the marzipan with a palette knife dipped in cold water to create a smooth finish (see pages 154–155). Add more icing and use the palette knife to lift it into soft peaks. Dust with icing sugar … and voilá!

Chocolate and orange Christmas cake

This cake is a great alternative to the traditional English Christmas cake. It's still packed full of luscious dried fruits and festive spices, but benefits from the delicious addition of orange liqueur and rich dark chocolate.

Serves 8
Preparation time: 1 day soaking,
    + 25 minutes
Cooking time: 2–2½ hours

200g (7oz) golden raisins
200g (7oz) seedless sultanas
100ml (3½fl oz) orange liqueur, plus extra
    for soaking
200g (7oz) unsalted butter, softened,
    plus extra for greasing
100g (3½oz) soft dark brown sugar
50g (2oz) molasses sugar
3 large eggs
150g (5oz) plain flour
175g (6oz) good-quality dark chocolate
    (about 70% cocoa solids), broken
    into pieces
1 tsp ground mixed spice
½ tsp ground cinnamon
½ tsp freshly grated nutmeg
juice of 1 lemon
100g (3½oz) chopped mixed peel
50g (2oz) whole glacé cherries
75g (2¾oz) walnut halves
75g (2¾oz) whole hazelnuts, roasted

For the decoration
2-3 tbsp apricot jam, sieved
mixed glacé fruits (orange slices, apricot,
    cherries etc)
mixed nuts (walnuts, pecans, pistachios)
gold leaf (optional)

Put the raisins and sultanas into a bowl and cover with half the orange liqueur. Cover the bowl and set aside for 24 hours.

When ready to bake, preheat the oven to 150°C (fan 130°C)/300°F/gas mark 2. Grease a 20cm (8in) springform cake tin.

In a large bowl, cream together the butter and sugars, using an electric hand whisk, until the mixture is light, pale and fluffy. Add the eggs, one at a time, continuing to whisk. If the mixture looks like it is going to split, add a small amount of the flour.

Put the chocolate pieces in a heatproof bowl that fits over a pan of gently simmering water (the base must not touch the water), and stir until it melts. Leave to cool slightly.

Add the cooled melted chocolate to the egg mixture. Sift in the flour, mixed spice, cinnamon and nutmeg, and fold in so that everything is well combined. Then add the lemon juice and remaining measured orange liqueur and mix together. Finally, mix in the soaked raisins, and sultanas, mixed peel, cherries, walnuts and hazelnuts.

Spoon the mix into the prepared tin. Level the surface and cover with a piece of baking paper. Bake for 2–2½ hours, depending on your oven. Test to see whether the cake is cooked by inserting a thin metal skewer into the centre: if it comes out clean, the cake is done.

Cool the cake in its tin on a wire rack, then remove from the tin, and peel off the lining paper. Feed the cake regularly with orange liqueur. I do this by carefully pouring straight from the bottle, but if you prefer, use a small ladle. Wrap the cake in clingfilm until ready to decorate. This cake is best eaten within three weeks.

To decorate, warm the apricot jam in a small pan and, using a pastry brush, glaze the top all over. Arrange the nuts and fruit on top and glaze these too. If you like, highlight with gold leaf for an extra special touch.

1

2

5

6

8

3

4

7

9

10

Christmas cake (my way)

If you're more of a purist when it comes to your Christmas cake, this recipe is the one for you. It's packed with dried fruit and roasted nuts, and, of course, delicious French brandy!

Serves 8

Preparation time: overnight soaking,
  + 25 minutes

Cooking time: 3½–4 hours

350g (12oz) golden sultanas

350g (12oz) raisins

300ml (10fl oz) brandy, plus extra for
  feeding

350g (12oz) unsalted butter, plus extra
  for greasing

200g (7oz) good-quality dark chocolate
  (about 70% cocoa solids), broken
  into pieces

200g (7oz) soft dark brown sugar

100g (3 ½ oz) molasses sugar

4 large eggs

300g (11oz) plain flour, sifted

2 tsp ground mixed spice

1 tsp ground cinnamon

finely grated zest and juice of 3 lemons

150g (5oz) chopped mixed peel

100g (3½oz) glacé cherries

50g (2oz) walnut halves

50g (2oz) shelled whole hazelnuts,
  roasted (see Tip page 17)

Soak the sultanas and raisins in about 150ml (5fl oz) of the brandy in a covered bowl overnight.

Preheat the oven to 150°C (fan 130°C)/300°F/gas mark 2. Grease a 20cm (8in) diameter deep cake tin with extra butter and double-line the base and side with enough baking paper that the paper stands a little above the side of the tin.

Put the chocolate pieces in a heatproof bowl that fits over a pan of gently simmering water (the base must not touch the water), and stir until it melts. Leave to cool slightly.

In the bowl of your blender/processor, using the power beater attachment, cream the measured butter and the sugars together at high speed until the mixture is light, pale and fluffy. Add the melted chocolate and then the eggs, mixing them in at a slower speed. (Add a little flour if the mixture looks like it may split.) Scrape down the side of the bowl occasionally, and mix until everything is incorporated and well blended.

Sift on the flour and spices, followed by another 150ml (5fl oz) of the brandy along with the lemon zest and juice. Mix together well then stir in the fruit and nuts gently, without breaking up the cherries or walnuts.

When combined well, spoon into the prepared tin and level the surface. Cover the top with a disc of baking paper and bake in the preheated oven for 3½–4 hours or until a thin-bladed knife inserted in the centre comes out clean.

Let the cake cool down in the tin, and then turn it out on to a wire rack. Peel off the lining paper and pour on the rest of the brandy while still warm. When cold, add some more brandy to taste, then wrap in clingfilm and store in a cool, dry place until ready to be decorated. This cake can be stored in an airtight tin for up to six months – but make sure you feed it regularly with brandy. When you're ready, decorate it using the royal icing recipe on page 219 and following the instructions on page 147 and photographs overleaf.

1

2

5

6

3

4

7

8

Ale fruit loaf

This is a very simple recipe, but so tasty. Our kitchen is next to the Young's brewery, where they make a special ale with roasted cocoa beans. This is the perfect partner for this recipe, but any good local ale will work too.

Serves 8
Preparation time: overnight soaking,
   + 10 minutes
Cooking time: 1¼ hours

390g (13½oz) mixed dried fruit
1 x 250ml bottle strong beer or ale
unsalted butter, for greasing
100g (3½oz) soft dark brown sugar
85g (3oz) self-raising flour
100g (3½oz) wholemeal self-raising flour
3 tsp ground mixed spice
2 eggs, beaten

Put the dried fruit into a large pan and cover with the bottled beer.

Gently heat the fruit until the beer is hot, but not boiling. Remove from the heat, cover and leave overnight.

When you are ready to cook the loaf, preheat the oven to 140°C (fan 120°C)/275°F/gas mark 1 and grease a 25 x 11cm (10 x 4¼in) loaf tin with butter.

Add the sugar, flours, mixed spice and eggs to the fruit mixture. Stir well until all the ingredients are combined.

Pour the mixture into the prepared loaf tin. Bake in the preheated oven for 1¼ hours until risen, pale brown and firm to the touch.

Cover with a tea-towel and leave on a wire rack to cool, still in its tin.

Remove from the tin and wrap the loaf tightly in clingfilm. Keep in a cool, dry place for up to six weeks. This loaf is delicious toasted and buttered with raspberry jam or served with a piece of Wensleydale cheese.

Chocolate and chestnut yule log

In France there is no Christmas pudding or cake during the festive season; instead, you will find a variety of Christmas logs. This is my favourite.

Serves 6

Preparation time: about 1 hour

Cooking time: 10 minutes

For the sponge

3 egg whites

130g (4¾oz) caster sugar

4 egg yolks

50g (2oz) unsalted butter, melted

100g (3½oz) plain flour

2 tsp baking powder

50ml (2fl oz) dark rum

For the chestnut cream

100ml (3½fl oz) double cream

400g (14oz) crème de marrons (sweet chestnut purée or spread, available from good supermarkets and suppliers)

For the chocolate glaze

150g (5oz) dark chocolate, broken into pieces

50g (2oz) unsalted butter

2 tbsp icing sugar

For the decoration

chocolate shavings

a few marrons glacés, halved

icing sugar, for dusting

Preheat the oven to 220°C (fan 200°C)/425°F/gas mark 7. Cover a baking sheet with silicone paper or a silicone rubber mat.

To start the sponge, beat the egg whites until stiff with an electric hand whisk, then gradually add 50g (2oz) of the sugar.

In a separate bowl, beat the egg yolks with the remaining sugar until the mixture is fluffy and white. Stir in the melted butter.

Sift the flour with the baking powder into the egg yolk mixture, then fold all the ingredients together. Mix in a little of the whipped egg white, then gently fold in the remainder.

Spread the mixture on to the silicone on the baking sheet with a palette knife, rather like making a Swiss roll. Bake in the preheated oven for 10 minutes, but you must keep an eye on it, as it cooks fast!

When out of the oven, cover the sponge with a damp tea-towel to stop it drying out and leave to cool completely.

To make the chestnut cream, in a large bowl, using an electric hand whisk, beat the cream to soft peaks, then fold in the *crème de marrons*.

To construct the cake, firstly soak the sponge with the dark rum, using a pastry brush. Spread the chestnut cream on to the sponge with a palette knife, then, using the silicone paper or mat, gently roll the filled sponge up nice and tight. Place on a serving plate, join down, and cut the ends at an angle. Save one of these ends to use as a 'branch' when glazing with the chocolate glaze.

Now make the chocolate glaze. Melt the chocolate in a bain-marie (see page 198), stirring occasionally, then stir in the butter and sugar. Leave to cool down.

Using a palette knife, cover the whole log with the chocolate glaze. Cover the saved end with glaze too, and stick it on top to mimic a branch. Using a fork, decorate all over for a wood effect. Place a few chocolate shavings or fans and *marrons glacés* on top, and dust with icing sugar.

Bon Noël!

1

2

5

6

3

4

7

8

Cheesecakes

Cheesecakes

The cheesecake comes in two basic styles: baked and unbaked. But there are more variations, depending on the region the dish comes from.

All classic cheesecakes have a base made from crushed biscuits and butter, but you can vary the biscuits. I use the classic digestive, gingernuts, amaretti and even chocolate bourbons in my recipes.

Cheesecakes consist of a mixture of cheese (although occasionally you find a 'cheesecake' containing no actual cheese, such as the Key Lime cheesecake in this chapter), eggs, cream, sugar and flavourings. The cheese can vary, but is usually cream cheese or mascarpone, and the cream is likely to be whipping cream or soured cream.

It is important to use the best cheese you can find – for the sake of the texture as well as the flavour of your cheesecake. And be sure to whip up your cheesecake really well, in order to incorporate as much air as possible and get a light texture.

Baked blueberry cheesecake

This recipe is very versatile and easy. You can replace the blueberries with raspberries or mixed berries. By adding a few drops of lemon oil and some finely grated lemon zest, you will give it a zesty note. Don't worry if the top cracks when the cake is cooling; this is part of the charm.

Serves 8

Preparation time: 30 minutes, + resting and chilling

Cooking time: about 1 hour

For the base

100g (3½oz) digestive biscuits

100g (3½oz) gingernut biscuits

50g (2oz) unsalted butter

For the filling

25g (1oz) cornflour

200g (7oz) caster sugar

600g (1lb 5oz) light soft cheese

1 vanilla pod, split

2 eggs

300ml (10fl oz) soured cream

For the topping

85g (3oz) caster sugar

50ml (2fl oz) water

400g (14oz) fresh blueberries

Tip

For an even biscuit crumb base, tip the crumbs into the bottom of the cake tin. Use the back of a spoon to gently push the crumbs from the centre outwards, until the base is smooth and level.

Preheat the oven to 180°C (fan 160°C)/350°F/gas mark 4. Line the base of a 20cm (8in) springform cake tin with baking paper.

Crush the biscuits into crumbs by whizzing in a food processor, or put in a plastic bag and crush with a rolling pin. Place in a bowl. Melt the butter and stir into the biscuits. Press the biscuit mix into the base of the prepared cake tin (see Tip below). Bake in the preheated oven for 10 minutes, then leave to cool down.

For the filling, mix together the cornflour and sugar in a large bowl. Beat in the soft cheese, the seeds from the vanilla pod, then the eggs. Finally, stir in the soured cream.

Pour this mixture into the cake tin, and level the top with a palette knife. Bake in the preheated oven for 10 minutes, then reduce the temperature to 140°C (fan 120°C)/275°F/gas mark 1, and bake for another 35–45 minutes until there is still a slight wobble to the centre. Switch off the oven, keep the door closed for 2 hours, then chill the cheesecake well.

To make the blueberry topping, place the sugar in a saucepan. Add the water and bring to the boil. When the sugar has dissolved, add the blueberries. Cover and cook for a few minutes, then cool.

Loosen the edge of the cheesecake, remove the tin and lining paper, then transfer to a serving plate. Spoon the blueberries over the cheesecake just before serving.

Ricotta, apple and cinnamon cheesecake

This cheesecake is a bit of an unusual one! The flavour of the filling is classic Italian – using succulent ricotta cheese – but it is presented on an American-style biscuit base. I like eating mine warm from the oven, as this enhances the delicious apple flavour.

Serves 4
Preparation time: 30 minutes
Cooking time: about 1½ hours

For the base
200g (7oz) digestive biscuits
75g (2¾oz) unsalted butter, melted,
  plus extra for greasing

For the filling
2 Cox's apples
25g (1oz) unsalted butter
1 tbsp Calvados
900g (2lb) ricotta cheese
150g (5oz) caster sugar
50g (2oz) plain flour
6 eggs, beaten
¼ tsp ground cinnamon
2 tsp vanilla extract

For the topping
1 large dessert apple
25g (1oz) soft light brown sugar
¼ tsp ground cinnamon

Preheat the oven to 180°C (fan 160°C)/350°F/gas mark 4. Grease a loose-based 22cm (8½in) springform cake tin with extra butter, then base-line with baking paper.

For the base, blitz the digestives in a food processor, or crumb with a rolling pin, and mix in a bowl with the melted butter. Press the biscuit mix evenly into the base of the prepared tin.

Bake in the preheated oven for 10 minutes until the base is lightly browned and just set. Remove from the oven and allow to cool for at least 5 minutes.

Reduce the temperature of the oven to 170°C (fan 150°C)/325°F/gas mark 3.

For the filling, peel and core the apples and cut in small cubes. Melt the butter in a small frying pan, and sauté the apple cubes until they are a nice colour. Pour the Calvados into the pan, and set it alight to flambé the apples. Leave to cool.

Place the ricotta in a large mixing bowl and stir it as smooth as possible with a spatula. Stir the caster sugar and flour thoroughly into the ricotta, then mix in the eggs, one at a time. Blend in the cinnamon and vanilla, then stir in the cooked apple. Pour the mixture into the prepared cake tin.

For the topping, peel and core the apple and cut into thin slices. Arrange gently on top of the mixture. Sprinkle the brown sugar and cinnamon over them.

Bake in the centre of the preheated oven for about 1¼ hours until the cake is a deep golden colour. Make sure the centre is fairly firm and the point of a sharp knife inserted in the centre comes out clean.

Cool on a wire rack. It will sink slightly as it cools. Cover, and chill until serving time.

Key lime pie cheesecake

This is my own cheese-free version of the Florida favourite. It should be white, not made with food colouring – as they say in Key West, 'if it's green, don't touch it'!

Serves 8–10
Preparation time: 1 day in advance for the
    poached lime slices, + about
    35 minutes, + chilling
Cooking time: 35–45 minutes

For the poached lime slices
125g (4½oz) caster sugar
125ml (4fl oz) water
1 x 30g packet fresh mint
4 limes, finely sliced

For the base
350g (12oz) digestive biscuits, crushed
    into crumbs
125g (4½oz) unsalted butter, melted, plus
    extra for greasing

For the filling
4 large eggs, separated
1 x 400ml tin full-fat condensed milk
finely grated zest and juice of 4 limes
50g (2oz) caster sugar

For the topping
150ml (5fl oz) whipping cream
icing sugar, for dusting

The day before making the pie, prepare the poached lime slices for the decoration. Place the sugar in a pan with the water and bring to the boil. Simmer until the sugar has melted, then add half the mint leaves and all the lime slices. Poach the lime in this minty syrup for about 10 minutes, then leave to cool and infuse overnight.

To make the base, mix the biscuit crumbs with the melted butter and press into a buttered deep 25cm (10in) loose-bottomed, preferably fluted, tart tin. If you don't have one of the latter, use a springform tin of the same size and just press the crumbs two-thirds of the way up the side. Leave the base to rest for another hour in the fridge.

Preheat the oven to 180°C (fan 160°C)/350°F/gas mark 4.

Line the biscuit case with greaseproof paper and half-fill it with ceramic baking beans or uncooked dried beans. Bake in the preheated oven for 10–15 minutes. Remove the beans and cook for another 5 minutes until the base has darkened slightly in colour. Remove from the oven and cool.

For the filling, beat the egg yolks in a bowl until light and fluffy, then beat in the condensed milk and lime zest and juice. In another bowl, whisk the egg whites and caster sugar until firm, then gently fold into the lime mixture, using a large metal spoon.

Completely fill the biscuit case with the lime mixture and bake in the preheated oven, at the same temperature, for 20–25 minutes until set and lightly browned around the edges. Leave to cool. It will sink slightly, so don't worry.

Loosen the edges of the tart, remove the tin and transfer to a serving plate. Finally, whip the cream until it peaks, spoon into a piping bag, and pipe around the edge of the cold tart. Dust the top with icing sugar, then decorate with the poached lime slices and some of the syrup, discarding the cooked mint and adding the remaining fresh mint leaves.

1

2

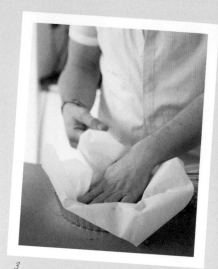

3

7

8

10

4

5

6

9

11

12

Lemon cheesecake with amaretti biscuits

This is a cold cheesecake with an Italian flair – I use amaretti biscuits and mascarpone cheese, which makes for a lovely creamy dessert.

Serves 4

Preparation time: 30 minutes, + chilling

For the base

100g (3½oz) amaretti biscuits, crushed into crumbs

50g (2oz) unsalted butter

For the filling

225g (8oz) mascarpone cheese

125ml (4fl oz) double cream, whipped to soft peaks

finely grated zest and juice of 1 lemon

50g (2oz) golden caster sugar

2 tsp lemon curd (for home-made, see Tip page 138)

For the topping

Fine strips of lemon zest

100g (3½oz) white chocolate, melted (see page 122)

Stand four 9cm (3½in) individual ring moulds or mousse rings on a baking sheet and line with acetate bands. (You can buy these from professional cook shops.)

Put the crushed biscuits into a mixing bowl. Melt the butter over a low heat and stir into the biscuit crumbs until well combined. Press the biscuit mixture into the base of the lined rings and put in the fridge to set.

Put the cheese into a bowl and beat it until soft and smooth. Add the cream, lemon zest and juice and the sugar, and mix well. Spread this mixture over the biscuit crumb bases, about halfway up the sides of the rings. Spoon a little lemon curd on top of each one and level off.

Put the rings in the fridge to chill for few hours, or freeze them.

Remove the cheesecakes from the rings and put on to plates. Decorate the tops with lemon zest, and drizzle on some melted white chocolate. You could also serve with a berry coulis (see page 92).

Tip

When crushing biscuits for bases, put them in a freezer bag and bash them with a rolling pin for a chunky texture. You could also use a food processor for a finer texture.

Chocolate cheesecake

This very rich cheesecake is great served with crème fraîche.

Serves 8
Preparation time: 30 minutes, + chilling
    and resting
Cooking time: about 1 hour

For the base
125g (4½oz) unsalted butter, melted,
    plus extra for greasing
250g (9oz) chocolate bourbon biscuits

For the filling
200g (7oz) full-fat cream cheese
400g (14oz) mascarpone cheese
75g (2¾oz) golden caster sugar
3 large eggs
40g (1½oz) pure cocoa powder, sifted,
    plus extra for dusting
100g (3½oz) good-quality dark chocolate,
    melted (see page 152)

Preheat the oven to 180°C (fan 160°C)/350°F/gas mark 4. Grease a 20cm (8in) springform cake tin with extra butter, and base-line with baking paper.

For the base, crush the bourbon biscuits into crumbs and place in a bowl. Pour over the melted butter. Mix together well, then press evenly into the prepared cake tin. Refrigerate for 30 minutes to an hour, until set.

For the filling, place the cream cheese, mascarpone and sugar in a food processor and blend until smooth. Next add the eggs, then the cocoa powder and lastly the melted chocolate, still beating. Continue beating until thoroughly combined.

Spoon the mixture on to the biscuit base in the tin. Level the surface, then bake in the preheated oven for about 50-60 minutes, or until the cheesecake still has a slight wobble in the centre. Turn off the oven and leave the cheesecake inside to cool and set for about 1 hour with the door closed. Take out of the oven, cool, then chill for at least 3 hours in the fridge.

Turn out of the tin, peel off the lining paper and transfer to a serving plate. Dust with cocoa and serve with crème fraîche.

Alternatives

Pecan or orange: You can add some chopped roasted pecan nuts, or even some finely grated orange zest to the mixture to give it a tangy flavour.

Mint: Another of my favourite ideas is to break up a handful of After Eight mint wafers into the mixture for a rich mint-chocolate flavour.

Pecan caramel cheesecake

This is the perfect cheesecake to indulge in during winter. The flavours – rich toffee and spicy biscuit base – marry perfectly to keep the chill at bay. The crunch of the roasted pecans gives an extra treat.

Serves 4
Preparation time: about 40 minutes,
   + resting and chilling
Cooking time: 45–55 minutes

For the base
75g (2¾oz) unsalted butter, plus extra
   for greasing
100g (3½oz) digestive biscuits
100g (3½oz) gingernut biscuits

For the roasted pecans
400g (14oz) shelled pecan nuts
85g (3oz) caster sugar

For the caramel
200g (7oz) caster sugar
75ml (2½fl oz) water
25g (1oz) unsalted butter

For the filling
25g (1oz) cornflour
200g (7oz) caster sugar
600g (1lb 5oz) light soft cheese
1 vanilla pod, split
2 large eggs
300g (11oz) soured cream

Preheat the oven to 180°C (fan 160°C)/350°F/gas mark 4. Grease the base of a 20cm (8in) springform cake tin, and base-line with baking paper.

Crush the biscuits into crumbs by whizzing in a food processor, or put in a plastic bag and crush with a rolling pin. Melt the butter and stir into the biscuits, then press evenly into the base of the prepared tin. Bake in the preheated oven for 10 minutes, then leave to cool down.

Place the pecans in a saucepan with the sugar, and on a gentle heat coat and roast them, stirring occasionally. This should take about 10 minutes, but do keep an eye on them! Leave to cool down, then divide into two portions.

Make the caramel by melting the sugar and water together in a saucepan. Heat gently until a nice dark golden colour. Remove from the heat, leave to cool down for 5 minutes, then add the butter.

For the filling, mix together the cornflour and sugar. Beat in the soft cheese, the seeds from the vanilla pod, then the eggs. Finally, stir in the soured cream and half the caramelized pecans.

Pour into the prepared tin. Swirl the caramel into the filling by running a knife through to create a marble effect. Bake in the preheated oven, at the same temperature, for 10 minutes. Then reduce the temperature to 90°C (fan 70°C)/194°F/the very lowest gas for 25–35 minutes. Switch off the oven and leave the cheesecake inside, door closed, for 2 hours. Chill well thereafter, preferably overnight.

Decorate the cheesecake with the rest of the caramelized pecans.

Tip

If the caramel sets while you are making the cheesecake, simply warm it gently in the pan to make it liquid again.

Raspberry swirl cheesecake

This is a rich recipe. You must make sure you use a good-quality preserve with lots of fruits. I prefer ones with the seeds, as they look more home-made.

Serves 6

Preparation time: 20 minutes, + resting and chilling

Cooking time: 45–50 minutes

For the base

200g (7oz) gingernut biscuits

50g (2oz) unsalted butter, melted, plus extra for greasing

2 tbsp caster sugar

For the filling

500g (1lb 2oz) cream cheese, softened

125g (4½oz) caster sugar

½ tsp vanilla extract

2 large eggs

75g (2¾oz) white chocolate, melted (see page 122)

3 tbsp raspberry preserve, melted

For the topping

fresh raspberries

Preheat the oven to 180°C (fan 160°C)/350°F/gas mark 4. Lightly grease a 20cm (8in) springform cake tin, and base-line with a circle of baking paper.

Crush the biscuits into crumbs by whizzing in a food processor, or put in a plastic bag and crush with a rolling pin. Melt the butter and stir into the biscuits along with the sugar. Firmly press into the bottom of the prepared cake tin. Bake in the preheated oven for 10 minutes, then leave to cool. Reduce the oven temperature to 140°C (fan 120°C)/275°F/gas mark 1.

For the filling, mix the cream cheese, sugar and vanilla until well blended. Add the eggs, and mix well, then stir in the melted chocolate.

Pour the filling into the cooled crust. Dot the melted raspberry preserve on top of the cheesecake with a spoon. Using the point of a knife, cut across the top of the cheesecake several times, creating a marbled effect.

Bake the cheesecake in the preheated oven for 35–40 minutes, or until the centre is almost set. Turn off the oven and leave to cool for 2 hours with the oven door closed.

Refrigerate the cheesecake for at least 3 hours. Loosen the edge of the cheesecake, remove the tin and lining paper and transfer to a serving plate. Decorate with fresh raspberries before serving.

Tip

Use good-quality cream cheese; it is definitely worth paying the price difference. The drier it is the better, and Philadelphia is fine.

Manhattan cheesecake

The king of cheesecakes, and every local café, restaurant or shop will have this traditional Big Apple classic. You can serve it with a variety of fruit compotes.

Serves 10–12
Preparation time: 20 minutes, + resting
  and chilling
Cooking time: 45 minutes

For the base
75g (2¾oz) unsalted butter, plus extra
  for greasing
300g (11oz) digestive biscuits, crushed

For the filling
1kg (2lb 4oz) cream cheese (the drier
  the better)
250g (9oz) caster sugar
3 tsp plain flour
1 tsp vanilla extract
finely grated zest and juice of 1 lemon
3 large eggs
300ml (10fl oz) soured cream

For the topping
150ml (5fl oz) soured cream
1 tbsp caster sugar
icing sugar, for dusting

Preheat the oven to 180°C (fan 160°C)/350°F/gas mark 4. Grease the base and side of a 23cm (9in) springform cake tin with extra butter, and line the base with baking paper.

For the base, melt the butter in a medium pan, then stir it into the biscuit crumbs. Press the mixture into the bottom of the prepared tin and bake in the preheated oven for 10 minutes. Cool on a wire rack while preparing the filling.

For the filling, increase the oven temperature to 220°C (fan 200°C)/425°F/gas mark 7.

In a mixer fitted with the paddle attachment, beat the cream cheese at medium-low speed until creamy, about 2 minutes, then gradually add the sugar, then the flour. Continue by adding the vanilla and lemon zest and juice, then whisk in the eggs, one at a time. Stir in the soured cream until well blended. The batter should be smooth, light and somewhat airy.

Pour the filling into the prepared tin. The top should be as smooth as possible. Bake in the preheated oven for 10 minutes. Reduce the oven temperature to 140°C (fan 120°C)/275°F/gas mark 1, and bake for 25 minutes more. If you gently shake the tin, the filling should have a slight wobble. Turn off the oven. Leave the cheesecake to cool in the oven for 2 hours, with the door closed. The cheesecake may get a slight crack on top as it cools.

For the topping, combine the soured cream and caster sugar. Spread over the cold cheesecake right to the edges, then refrigerate overnight. Dust with icing sugar before serving.

1

2

3

7

8

10

4

5

6

9

11

12

Puddings

Puddings

For me, the third course of a lunch or dinner meal is the most important one. It's the one everybody will remember, so it needs to make a good impression! This chapter is a small compilation of my favourite desserts – the ones I serve at home when I am entertaining. As well as tasting fabulous, they look great and some of them will add a bit of drama to the table when they are served. They're worth the hard work and preparation – treat yourself with a glass of champagne or dessert wine when you serve them!

Sticky toffee pudding in golden syrup tins

As a Frenchman, I was lucky enough to taste my first ever sticky toffee pudding at the famous Sharrow Bay Hotel in the Lake District. I have been a fan ever since, and this recipe is my version, cooked in golden syrup tins to wow your guests. It's a good idea to save up your tins so that you have plenty to hand for when you want to cook this recipe. Alternatively, golden syrup will keep well if you decant it into a Kilner jar and keep it in the cupboard for future use.

Serves 6
Preparation time: 15 minutes, + resting
Cooking time: 20–25 minutes

150g (5oz) chopped dates, soaked in
    125ml (4fl oz) hot tea for at least
    2 hours
375g (13oz) golden syrup
50g (2oz) unsalted butter, softened
150g (5oz) caster sugar
2 large eggs
a few drops of caramel extract (optional)
150g (5oz) plain flour
1 tsp baking powder

To serve
vanilla ice-cream

Preheat the oven to 180°C (fan 160°C)/350°F/gas mark 4.

Drain the dates. Measure out the golden syrup. If you haven't got six 454g golden syrup tins, you could use ramekins (see Tip below).

Make the pudding mix by whisking the butter and sugar together into a large bowl, using an electric hand whisk. Then add the eggs and mix in well. Add the caramel extract, if using, and the dates, then fold in the flour and baking powder gently.

Pour into each syrup tin 2 tbsp golden syrup and tilt the tins to coat the lower half and the base. Then divide the date mixture between the tins. Put the tins on a baking sheet.

Bake in the preheated oven for approximately 20–25 minutes.

Remove the baking sheet from the oven and allow the tins to cool for 5 minutes. Scoop a ball of vanilla ice-cream on top of each, and serve.

Tip

If you don't have golden syrup tins, ramekins will work just fine. You will need 6 large ramekins or 8 smaller ones and they should be filled to a maximum of three-quarters full.

Salted butter caramel mousse with mini pears

In the words of the great Michel Roux Junior, 'This is a favourite combination'. Of course, I recommend you use Brittany salted butter, to ensure the best possible flavour! This is a recipe for a special occasion, when you want to make more of an effort.

Serves 6

Preparation time: about an hour,
+ chilling

1 vanilla sponge cake, home-made (see page 16), or good-quality bought
2 medium pears, peeled, cored and sliced thinly
6 ready-prepared small baby pears from a jar or tin
1 tsp pure cocoa powder, for dusting

For the mousse

200g (7oz) caster sugar
50ml (2fl oz) water
500ml (18fl oz) milk
100g (3½oz) salted butter, plus extra for greasing
2 egg yolks, beaten
6 gelatine leaves, soaked in a little cold water (or 12g, but check packet instructions)
300ml (10fl oz) whipping cream or double cream, whipped

For the light caramel

200g (7oz) caster sugar
50ml (2fl oz) water

First, make a dark caramel for the mousse. Heat the sugar and water in a saucepan until the sugar has dissolved. Meanwhile, heat the milk in a separate saucepan.

Bring the sugar and water mixture to the boil, then boil without stirring until the syrup caramelizes, thickening and turning a dark caramel colour. To avoid crystallization, do not stir and wash down the crystals at the side of the pan (see Tip page 49).

Stir the butter into the caramel until melted, then add the warm milk, stirring thoroughly until the caramel has dissolved. Remove from the heat and gradually add half of it to the egg yolks, stirring, then mix in the rest. Return the mixture to a very low heat and heat gently, stirring constantly, until the mixture thickens to a custard.

Fold in the softened gelatine, mixing well. Leave the mixture to cool slightly, then cool further in the fridge, but don't let it set completely.

Gently fold the whipped cream, using a large metal spoon, into the chilled caramel mixture.

To assemble the desserts, take six circular deep moulds, about 9cm (3½ in) wide and 5.5cm (2¼in) deep. Cut out six discs of sponge cake using a circular cutter the same size as the moulds, and then slice through horizontally to about 1cm (½in) thick. Place a disc of sponge in the base of each mould. Top with a layer of mousse and a few pear slices. Top with another layer of mousse and a sponge disc. Place the moulds in the refrigerator overnight until set, or freeze.

For the caramel, place the sugar and water in a saucepan and heat until the sugar dissolves. Bring to the boil and cook without stirring until the syrup caramelizes and thickens to a pale golden colour.

Dip the small pears into the light caramel, coating them well, and leave to set on a plate (butter the plate first to prevent sticking).

Using a fork, drizzle any remaining caramel over six serving plates. Unmould the six mousses, and place on the serving plates. Dust with cocoa powder and serve with a caramel-coated pear.

Banoffee pie

I love everything about this pie – the crunchiness of the base and the richness of the filling are irresistible. I prefer to make this with slightly underripe bananas that have a bit of bite.

Serves 8-10
Preparation time: 40 minutes, + chilling
Cooking time: 10 minutes

For the base
75g (2¾oz) unsalted butter, plus
　1 tbsp melted for greasing
1 x 300g packet chocolate HobNobs

For the toffee filling
100g (3½oz) unsalted butter
100g (3½oz) soft dark brown sugar
1 x 397g tin condensed milk

For the topping
3 large bananas, slightly underripe
500ml (18fl oz) double cream
pure cocoa powder, for dusting

Grease a 22cm (8½in) ceramic flan dish with the melted butter. Place the HobNobs in a freezer bag and crush to crumbs with a rolling pin.

Gently melt the butter in a saucepan, then pour over the crushed biscuits, mixing until they bind together. Transfer to the dish and firmly pat with a spoon to cover the base. Place in the fridge to set.

To make the toffee filling, place the butter and sugar in a pan and heat gently until the sugar dissolves. Pour in the condensed milk and gently heat, stirring continuously until the mixture boils. Once the mixture has come to boiling point, remove from the heat and pour the toffee over the biscuit base. Place in the fridge to cool.

Once the pie has chilled, slice the bananas and arrange them on top of the toffee. Whip the cream to soft peaks and spoon or pipe on to cover the bananas. Finally, dust with cocoa powder and place in the fridge to chill before serving.

Hot gingerbread soufflé

This dessert contains all the flavour of traditional gingerbread, but is presented in a much lighter way. Don't be scared of soufflés – just remember that you have to make them just before you are ready to serve, and take them straight to the table to dazzle your guests!

Serves 8
Preparation time: 30 minutes
Cooking time: 11 minutes

50g (2oz) unsalted butter
135g (4¾oz) caster sugar
210g (7¼oz) dark or couverture chocolate
    (70% cocoa solids), broken into pieces
2 tsp ground ginger
1 tsp ground cinnamon
2 tsp dark rum
¼ tsp vanilla extract
5 eggs, separated

To serve
vanilla custard (for home-made
    see Tip page 196)

Preheat the oven to 180°C (fan 160°C)/350°F/gas mark 4. Melt half the butter and use to brush the inside of eight small ramekins. Tip 25g (1oz) of the caster sugar into one ramekin and tap around the sides to lightly coat. Pour the excess into the next ramekin and repeat until all the ramekins are butter- and sugar-coated.

Melt the chocolate with the spices, rum, vanilla extract and remaining butter in a large heatproof bowl over a pan of gently simmering water (the base of the bowl must not touch the water). Stir until smooth. Remove the bowl from the heat and mix the egg yolks in one at a time.

In a large clean bowl, whisk the egg whites to soft, moist-looking peaks, then add the remaining sugar. Mix a little into the chocolate mixture, then gently fold in the rest, using a large metal spoon.

Divide the soufflé mixture between the ramekins, spooning it in, and place the ramekins on a baking sheet. Bake in the preheated oven for exactly 11 minutes.

Serve with vanilla custard poured into the centre of each soufflé.

Tip

These soufflés must be cooked just before eating; they will flatten within 2 minutes of being removed from the oven. Be careful not to open the oven during cooking, as this may prevent them from rising.

1

2

5

6

3

4

7

8

Eggnog trifle

This is my spin on the traditional trifle, which is such a popular Christmas dessert. The recipe contains delicious amaretti biscuits and plenty of liqueur – it's Christmas in a glass.

Serves 6

Preparation time: 30 minutes, +
     macerating and chilling
Cooking time: 20 minutes

350g (12oz) mixed fresh berries, such as
     raspberries, blueberries and
     cranberries, plus extra to decorate
3 tbsp icing sugar, plus extra for dusting
3 tbsp Grand Marnier
12 soft amaretti biscuits, plus a few extra
     for topping
6 tbsp berry compote (home-made – see
     page 92 – or bought)
250g (9oz) mascarpone cheese
50g (2oz) caster sugar

For the eggnog custard

300ml (10fl oz) full-fat milk
2 large egg yolks
2 tbsp cornflour
2 tbsp caster sugar
3 tbsp Advocaat liqueur
¼ tsp vanilla extract

Stir the berries, icing sugar and Grand Marnier together in a bowl and leave to macerate for 20 minutes.

Divide the 12 amaretti biscuits between six glasses. Top each with 1 tbsp compote, then divide half the mixed fresh berries between the glasses.

In a bowl, mix the mascarpone and sugar together. Spoon this over the fruits, then chill for 30 minutes.

Meanwhile, make the eggnog custard. Put the milk in a pan and heat, but do not boil. Put the egg yolks, cornflour and sugar in a bowl and beat together well. Pour the warm milk over the egg mixture and whisk, using an electric hand whisk, until well combined. Return to the pan, and stir with a wooden spoon over a low heat until the mixture thickens. Do not let it boil.

Pour the custard into a bowl and stir in the Advocaat and vanilla. Put a piece of baking paper on the surface to prevent a skin forming, and leave to cool.

Spoon the custard over the mascarpone and top with the remaining berries and the extra amaretti biscuits, crumbled. Serve dusted with icing sugar.

Tip

Without the Advocaat liqueur added, the custard above is a basic vanilla custard, which you will find referred to occasionally throughout the book. To make it into a Calvados custard, for instance, replace the Advocaat with Calvados.

Choux Parisiens

The light choux pastry and the praline cream in this very traditional French gâteau make a great combination. This is best eaten on the day that it's made.

Serves 6–8
Preparation time: about 45 minutes
  + chilling
Cooking time: 35–40 minutes

For the choux
150g (5oz) plain flour
125ml (4fl oz) water
125ml (4fl oz) milk
100g (3½oz) unsalted butter, cut into
  small pieces
4 eggs, lightly beaten
40g (1½oz) flaked almonds

For the crème mousseline
3 egg yolks
100g (3½oz) caster sugar
60g (2¼oz) plain flour
250ml (9fl oz) milk
200g (7oz) unsalted butter, softened
100g (3½oz) chocolate and hazelnut
  spread (e.g. Nutella or Green & Blacks)
icing sugar, for dusting

Preheat the oven to 200°C (fan 180°C)/400°F/gas mark 6. Line a baking tray with baking paper, and draw a pencil circle around a 22cm (8½in) cake tin.

Sift the flour and place to one side. Heat the water and milk in a pan over a medium heat. Add the butter and when melted bring to a fast boil. Remove from the heat and immediately add all the flour. Working fast, return to the heat and beat vigorously with a wooden spoon until the mixture leaves the side of the pan and becomes smooth and shiny. This will take a minute or so.

Allow the mixture to cool for a couple of minutes, then add the eggs, a little at a time, beating well after each addition, before adding the next lot of egg. You will be left with a smooth and glossy mixture.

Spoon the mixture into a piping bag fitted with a large star tube. Following the circle you have drawn on the paper, pipe a ring on to the prepared tray. Then pipe a second ring on the inside of the first, positioning it so that they touch. Pipe a third ring on top of the first two. Sprinkle with the flaked almonds.

Place in the preheated oven and cook until risen and golden brown. Keep an eye on your pastry, but it will take about 35–40 minutes. Remove from the oven and cool on a wire rack.

To make the crème mousseline, put the egg yolks, sugar and flour in a large bowl and beat with an electric hand whisk for 3–4 minutes until pale and creamy.

Place the milk in a saucepan and bring to the boil. Strain the milk into the egg mixture, whisking until it is smooth. Pour the mixture back into the pan and, whisking all the time, bring to the boil. Cook gently for about 2 minutes, still whisking. Pour into a bowl and add half the unsalted butter, stirring to melt. Leave to cool.

Using an electric mixer, beat the remaining butter into the cool mixture, then the hazelnut spread. Chill in the fridge for 30 minutes.

When you are ready, place the choux pastry ring on a plate and slice it in half horizontally. Spoon the mousseline cream into a piping bag with a star tube. Pipe the cream over the bottom half of the ring. Place the other half on top and dust with icing sugar.

Hot chocolate fondants

For me this is the easiest, almost foolproof, chocolate fondant recipe. The secret's in the timing; don't guess. Set your kitchen timer and you'll be able to serve your friends the most tasty, warm, chocolatey dessert they've ever had. And an added bonus is that you can even prepare the fondants the day before!

Serves 4
Preparation time: 25 minutes
Cooking time: 8 minutes

125g (4½oz) unsalted butter, plus extra
    for greasing
1 tbsp pure cocoa powder, plus extra
    for dusting
125g (4½oz) dark chocolate, broken
    into pieces
60g (2¼oz) caster sugar
3 small eggs
3 small egg yolks
100g (3½oz) plain flour, sifted

Preheat the oven to 200°C (fan 180°C)/400°F/gas mark 6. Thoroughly butter four 200ml (7fl oz) ovenproof moulds (dariole moulds preferably), and dust lightly with the extra cocoa powder.

Melt the measured butter and the chocolate together in a large heatproof bowl over a pan of gently simmering water (the base of the bowl must not touch the water).

In a large bowl, using an electric hand whisk, beat together the sugar, eggs and egg yolks until light and pale.

Pour the melted butter and chocolate over the egg mix and then fold in the sifted flour and measured cocoa using a metal spoon.

Place the individual moulds on a baking sheet. Pour the mixture into the prepared moulds, and bake in the preheated oven for approximately 8 minutes.

When the outside is crisp to the touch, loosen the edges with a knife and carefully turn out of the moulds on to the serving plates. The centre should still be soft and lusciously saucy – just like me!

Serve with thick cream, crème fraîche or vanilla ice-cream.

Tips

These fondants can be made the day before and kept in the fridge to be cooked just before you are ready to eat them.

To check that the fondants are cooked, I suggest you make an extra one that you can dig into to test the texture.

Chocolate and cherry teardrops

This is not a 1970s Black Forest gâteau revival! This dessert has a deep, rich flavour and the teardrop shape adds a contemporary twist.

Serves 6
Preparation time: 40 minutes, + chilling

175g (6oz) dark chocolate (70% cocoa solids), broken into pieces
200g (7oz) bought chocolate sponge cake (or use the sponge on page 12)
4 large egg yolks
125g (4½oz) caster sugar
150g (5oz) unsalted butter
75g (2¾oz) pure cocoa powder
250ml (9fl oz) double cream

For the decoration
1 x 390g jar cherries in Kirsch, drained (reserve the syrup)
fresh cherries with stalks if in season (or use more cherries from a jar)
edible silver leaf

Place 100g (3½oz) of the chocolate in a heatproof bowl set over a pan of simmering water (the water must not touch the bowl), and melt gently, stirring occasionally.

Cut some acetate into six 30 x 5cm (12 x 2in) strips. With a sharp knife cut six teardrop shapes out of the chocolate sponge (see the Tip below): about 1.5cm (5/8in) thick, 7.5cm (3in) wide and 10cm (4in) long (large enough for the acetate to wrap around). Brush one side of each acetate strip thickly with the melted chocolate. Shape around the sponge teardrops (with the chocolate on the inside), and secure with a paperclip. Place on a baking sheet, and leave to set in the fridge.

In a large bowl, using an electric hand whisk, beat the egg yolks and sugar together until thick and pale.

Melt the butter with the cocoa and remaining chocolate in a heatproof bowl set over a pan of simmering water, stirring occasionally (don't let the bowl touch the water). Fold the melted chocolate mixture into the egg mixture. Lightly whisk the cream in a bowl, then fold it into the chocolate mixture to make a mousse.

Spoon a layer of drained cherries into the teardrops (on top of the sponge) and drizzle each teardrop with 2 tsp of the cherry syrup. Pipe or spoon the mousse on top. Chill for 1 hour.

Carefully unpeel the acetate from the teardrops. Decorate with more cherries and some silver leaf.

Tip

How to cut the teardrop-shaped sponge base: Curve one piece of acetate into a teardrop shape (as per the size above), and paperclip the ends together. Put this over the sponge, and cut closely around on the inside. Use this sponge shape as a template for cutting the others. And if you can't get hold of acetate, use a new plastic folder, cut into strips – or a double thickness of baking paper or parchment.

Apple Charlotte

There's a lot of controversy over who created this classic dish – was it British, French or Russian? It really doesn't matter, when done well it's a perfect winter warmer. My favourite way to serve it is with Calvados custard.

Serves 8

Preparation time: about 40 minutes,
  + cooling and resting
Cooking time: about 45 minutes

450g (1lb) apples (half Bramley and half
  Cox's makes a good mix)
1 tbsp caster sugar
200g (7oz) unsalted butter
10 slices bread taken from a large loaf
  (they should be about 5mm/¼in thick)
1 egg yolk
2 extra apples, peeled, cored and diced
  into 1cm (½in) cubes
100g (3½oz) soft light brown sugar

To serve

custard (for home-made see
  Tip page 196)

Peel and core the apples, then slice into thin rings. Rinse in a bowl of cold water, then transfer to a pan along with the caster sugar and 30g (1¼oz) of the butter. Cook over a low heat until they are just soft enough to beat into a purée. Beat the apples until smooth, then set aside to cool.

Remove the crusts from the bread, then melt the remaining butter very gently in a small pan. Cut each slice of bread into two rectangles and brush each piece with melted butter on both sides. Use three-quarters of these to line the base and sides of a 600ml (1 pint) pudding basin or Charlotte mould. Make certain you overlap the bread pieces a little so you don't leave any gaps, and press down firmly to seal.

When the apple purée has cooled completely, beat the egg yolk into it. Tip a third of the purée into the bread-lined bowl, then top with half the diced apple. Top with a layer of bread, and sprinkle with half the brown sugar. Repeat this once more, then finish with the final third of the apple purée. Now seal the top with the remaining butter-soaked bread. Cover the bread with a plate that's slightly smaller than the bowl and weigh down with a 1kg (2lb 4oz) weight. Set aside to compress for 30 minutes.

Meanwhile, preheat the oven to 200°C (fan 180°C)/400°F/gas mark 6.

After 30 minutes, transfer the bowl (with the weight still on it) to the preheated oven and bake for about 35 minutes. Carefully remove the weight and the plate, and bake the pudding for a further 10 minutes or until browned on top. Remove from the oven and allow to settle in the basin for a few minutes.

Invert the pudding on to a warmed serving plate, and serve immediately with custard.

Pink champagne jelly with berries

This is nothing like your childhood jelly; it's a grown-up version. You can replace the champagne with a dessert wine for a sweeter version.

Serves 8

Preparation time: 20 minutes
+ chilling and setting overnight

350g (12oz) small fresh strawberries
225g (8oz) fresh raspberries
250g (9oz) mixed fresh red, white and
blackcurrants
425ml (15fl oz) pink champagne
1 vanilla pod, split
6 gelatine leaves, soaked in water (check
individual packet instructions)
1 tsp lemon juice

First, prepare the berries by rinsing them and removing the stalks. Halve the strawberries and mix all the fruit together in a bowl.

In a saucepan, heat half the champagne with the vanilla pod to simmering point. Strain the soaked gelatine, then whisk into the champagne. Make sure everything has dissolved before stirring in the remaining champagne and the lemon juice. Pour the liquid into a jug and allow to cool.

Take a 900g (2lb) loaf tin and lay half the prepared fruit in the base. Remove the vanilla pod and pour half the jelly mixture over the fruit. Place the tin in the fridge for a couple of hours until it begins to set.

After the first layer has begun to set, place the remaining berries in the tin and pour over the remaining jelly mixture. Place in the fridge to set overnight.

When you are ready to serve the jelly, dip the base of the tin briefly in hot water. Turn out on to a plate. Use a sharp knife, also dipped in hot water, to cut your jelly into slices.

This tastes great served with marscapone cheese or crème fraîche.

Blancmange with pears

I know most people hate blancmange, but a revival is around the corner. Give this one a try and you will be convinced!

Serves 8

Preparation time: 45 minutes, + infusing
   overnight, chilling and setting
Cooking time: 10 minutes

For the poached pears and jelly

4 firm pears

1 litre (1¾ pints) water

juice of 1 lemon

300g (11oz) caster sugar

275g (9½oz) clear runny honey

a grinding of black pepper

1 vanilla pod, split

1 cinnamon stick

3 cloves

2 star anise

8 gelatine leaves, soaked in water (check
   individual packet instructions)

For the blancmange

750ml (a good 1¼ pints) full-fat milk

125g (4½oz) ground almonds

1 vanilla pod, split

1 tsp almond essence

8 gelatine leaves, soaked in water (check
   individual packet instructions)

2 egg yolks

100g (3½oz) caster sugar

Tip

To help release the jelly and blancmange, place the bottom of the mould briefly in a sink of hot water.

The day before, poach the pears. Peel and core the pears, but keep them whole and retain the stalk. Place them in a pan with the water, lemon juice, sugar, honey, black pepper, vanilla and spices. Bring to the boil and cook for 10 minutes or until the pears can be pierced easily with a sharp knife. Remove from the heat and leave the flavours to infuse overnight.

The following day, strain the pears and syrup. Keep 150ml (5fl oz) of the syrup: this will make the glaze when you are ready to serve.

Strain the gelatine leaves, then place them in a pan with the rest of the pear syrup and heat gently until dissolved. Pour half the jelly mixture into the bottom of a 1.5 litre (2¾ pint) ring mould and place in the fridge so that it begins to set. This will take a couple of hours.

Once the jelly at the bottom of the mould has begun to set, take the poached pears and cut them lengthways into slices, about 1cm (½in) thickness. Place the poached pear slices on top of the set jelly and then pour the remaining pear jelly mixture over the top. (If it has set, you will need to warm it through gently over the hob.) Place in the fridge to set for a few hours.

Meanwhile, prepare the blancmange. In a saucepan, bring the milk to the boil, then remove from the heat. Add the ground almonds and vanilla pod and leave to infuse for a few hours.

Once the jelly has set, pass the milk and almond mixture through a sieve into a clean pan. Discard the ground almonds and vanilla pod. Add the almond essence to the milk, and then heat gently until hot. Remove from the heat. Drain the soaked gelatine leaves, add to the hot milk and stir to dissolve.

In a bowl, using an electric hand whisk, whip the egg yolks and sugar together until pale. Slowly pour the warm milk over the top and mix thoroughly. Transfer the mixture to a jug and leave to cool.

Once cooled, pour the blancmange mixture over the pear jelly and place in the fridge to set overnight.

When you are ready to serve the blancmange, reduce the reserved pear liquid to a syrupy glaze. Remove the blancmange from the mould, place on a plate and cover with the pear syrup.

Chocolate bread and butter pudding

I created this warming pudding when I had some left over *pain au chocolat*. It's much more exciting than regular bread and butter pudding, and a drop of Amaretto or Cointreau will make it even more special.

Serves 4–6
Preparation time: 20 minutes
Cooking time: 30–40 minutes

unsalted butter, for greasing
4 standard-size pains au chocolat
50g (2oz) golden sultanas
450ml (16fl oz) full-fat milk
150g (5oz) dark chocolate (70 per
    cent cocoa solids), broken into pieces
3 eggs
1 tsp vanilla extract
1 tbsp caster sugar, plus extra
    for sprinkling

Preheat the oven to 170°C (fan 150°C)/325°F/Gas 3, and grease a 1.2 litre (2 pint) serving dish with butter.

Cut the *pains au chocolat* in half horizontally and then into quarters – triangles or squares. Arrange 12 of the quarters in layers in your serving dish, sprinkling the sultanas between each layer. Reserve four of the quarters for the top, so that your final layer is *pain au chocolat*.

Place the milk and chocolate in a saucepan and heat gently so that the chocolate melts and the mixture becomes hot, but do not allow to boil.

In a large bowl, mix the eggs, vanilla and sugar, then add the hot chocolate milk and mix until well combined.

Gently pour this over the *pain au chocolat* and sultanas, being careful not to dislodge the top layer of *pain au chocolat*. Leave to stand for 10 minutes.

Sprinkle a little extra caster sugar over the top and bake in the preheated oven for 30–40 minutes until the top is brown and crisp.

Tip

The day before, place the sultanas in dark rum and soak overnight for added grown-up flavour!

Chocolate crème brûlée

This is a very rich version of the popular bistro dessert, so keep the meal light.

Serves 6
Preparation time: 25 minutes, + cooling
   and chilling
Cooking time: about 15 minutes

85g (3oz) dark chocolate, broken
   into pieces
5 egg yolks
300g (11oz) caster sugar
300ml (10fl oz) double cream
1 vanilla pod, split

For the topping
300g (11oz) demerara sugar

Melt the chocolate in a heatproof bowl suspended above a pan of simmering water, stirring occasionally. Remove from direct heat.

Whisk the egg yolks and sugar together in a bowl, using an electric hand whisk, until white and fluffy.

Place the cream and the vanilla pod in a heavy-based saucepan and bring to boiling point.

Whisking constantly, add the hot cream mixture to the whisked egg yolks. Mix together well, then pour back into the saucepan. Cook gently, stirring constantly, until the mixture thickens slightly. Remove the vanilla pod.

Pour the cream mixture over the melted chocolate and fold together.

Pour the chocolate mixture into four ramekins about 15cm (6in) in diameter and 3cm (1¼in) deep. Cool, then chill for a few hours until set, or overnight.

Sprinkle the demerara sugar finely and evenly over the set brûlée. Sprinkle with a little water then, using a chef's blow-torch, caramelize the sugar topping on each. Alternately, preheat the grill and caramelize the chocolate brûlées under the grill. Serve straightaway.

Tip

When creating a sugar crust, use a blow-torch if you can. If you don't have one use the grill. Put the ramekins close to the heat (keep an eye on them) so that the crust browns quickly; otherwise there is a danger of overcooking the custard. If you cook the crème brûlée the day before you plan to eat it, and keep it in the fridge overnight, the custard will be cold when it goes under the grill, so there will be less danger of it overcooking. Use demerara sugar on the top, as white sugar burns more easily.

Fusion crème brûlée

It's funny how the French and British always fight about who created this – 'burned cream' or 'créme brûlée'?! This is my own, Asian-inspired version.

Serves 6

Preparation time: 15 minutes, + cooling
    and setting
Cooking time: 40–45 minutes

1 piece fresh root ginger, about
    100g (3½oz)
2 stems lemongrass, outer leaves
    removed
350ml (12fl oz) double cream
125ml (4fl oz) full-fat milk
1 vanilla pod, split
6 large eggs
100g (3½oz) caster sugar

For the topping

300g (11oz) demerara sugar

Preheat the oven to 140°C (fan 120°C)/275°F/gas mark 1. Have ready a shallow dish – about 15cm (6in) in diameter and 3cm (1¼in) deep – or 6 smaller individual ones.

Put the root ginger and lemongrass in a food processor and zap them to a paste.

Put the cream, milk, split vanilla pod and the lemongrass and ginger paste into a large saucepan. Heat slowly until hot, but not boiling.

Beat the eggs and sugar together in a bowl, using an electric hand whisk, until white and fluffy. Slowly pour the hot cream over the egg mixture, mixing continuously.

Strain the mixture through a fine mesh sieve into your shallow dish or dishes. Bake in the preheated oven for approximately 40–45 minutes or until the mixture is wobbly.

Leave to cool down, then chill for a few hours until set, or overnight.

When you are ready to serve, sprinkle the demerara sugar evenly over the top and caramelize with a blow-torch. Alternately, preheat the grill and caramelize the brûlées under the grill. Serve straightaway.

Pastries & biscuits

Puff pastry

This is the king of pastries, and the flavour and texture when baked are worth all the effort.

Makes 1kg (2lb 4oz)
Preparation time: 2 x overnight
    chilling and resting, + about 3 hours,
    including chilling
Cooking time: see individual recipes

400g (14oz) plain flour, plus extra
    for dusting
1–1½ tsp salt
90g (3¼oz) cold unsalted butter, cut
    into small pieces
210ml (just over 7fl oz) cold water
300g (11oz) unsalted butter, softened
1 large egg yolk, beaten with 1 tbsp milk,
    for egg-wash

Tips

Make sure you dust any loose flour away from the pastry, as it can prevent the puff pastry from rising properly when baked.

Roll the pastry without pushing too hard, otherwise you will break all the lovely layers you made when creating the turns.

As puff pastry contains no egg or sugar it needs to be brushed with an egg-wash before baking.

Sift the flour and salt into a large bowl. Rub the butter into the flour, using your fingertips. Work quickly, to keep the dough cold. It will be quite sticky. Make a well in the centre and add all the water at once. Using a rubber spatula or your fingers, gradually draw the flour into the water. Mix until all the flour is incorporated. Do not knead.

Turn the dough out on to a lightly floured surface, and knead it a few times, rounding it into a ball. Wrap it in clingfilm and chill overnight.

Place the softened butter between two sheets of clingfilm. Use a rolling pin to roll it into a rectangle 12.5 x 20cm (4¾ x 8in). The dough and butter must be of almost equal consistency. If necessary, let the dough sit at room temperature to soften, or chill the butter to harden.

On a lightly floured board, roll the dough into a rectangle 30 x 37.5cm (12 x 14¾in). Using a pastry brush, remove any flour from the surface.

Peel one piece of clingfilm from the butter. Position the butter in the centre of the dough and remove the remaining clingfilm. Fold the four edges of the dough over the butter; stretch it if necessary, as none of the butter must be exposed. With the folded side up, press the dough several times with a rolling pin. Use a rocking motion to create ridges. Put the rolling pin in each ridge and slowly roll to widen it. Repeat until all the ridges are doubled in size. Using the ridges as a starting point, roll the dough into a smooth, even rectangle 20 x 50cm (8 x 20in). Keep the corners of the dough as right angles.

Fold the dough in thirds lengthways, like a business letter. This completes the first turn. Rotate the dough 90 degrees so that the folded edge is on your left and the dough faces you like a book. Roll out again, repeating the ridging technique. Again, the dough should be in a smooth, even rectangle of 20 x 50cm (8 x 20in). Fold the dough in thirds again, completing the second turn. Cover the dough with clingfilm and chill for at least 30 minutes.

Repeat the rotating, rolling and folding until the dough has had five turns. Do not perform more than two turns without a resting and chilling period. Cover the dough and chill overnight before shaping and baking. Remember to chill after shaping, for about 30 minutes.

Brush with egg-wash and bake at 200ºC (fan 180ºC)/400ºF/gas mark 6. The timing will depend on the shape and size of the pastry.

1

2

3

4

5

6

7

8

9

Choux pastry

Funnily enough, this is the pastry everybody thinks is difficult to make, but don't worry. In reality, it is very simple and fast, and doesn't require much in the way of ingredients or equipment. The only thing that might need a bit of practice is the piping needed to create the best éclairs or profiteroles.

Makes 300g (11oz)
Preparation time: 20–30 minutes
Cooking time: 15–20 minutes

80ml (a good 2½fl oz) water
40g (1½oz) unsalted butter, at room temperature, cut into cubes, plus extra for greasing
50g (2oz) plain flour, sifted
2 eggs, at room temperature

Place the water and butter in a medium saucepan over a medium heat. Cook, stirring with a wooden spoon, for 3–4 minutes or until the butter melts and the mixture is just coming to the boil.

Add all the flour to the butter mixture at once and use a wooden spoon to beat until well combined. Place over a low heat and cook, stirring, for 1–2 minutes or until the mixture forms a ball and begins to come away from the side of the saucepan. Set aside for 5 minutes to cool slightly.

Whisk one of the eggs in a small bowl and set aside. Whisk the remaining egg in a second small bowl, then add it to the flour mixture, beating well with a wooden spoon. Gradually add the reserved egg, bit by bit, and beat until the mixture just falls from the spoon but still holds its shape (you will only need about half the egg).

Spoon the pastry or pipe it (using a large piping bag fitted with a 1cm/½in plain tube) on to a buttered baking sheet to the required shapes and sizes, and brush them with a bit of the remaining egg to give them a nice golden colour when baked. (You can make them any size or shape – mini éclairs or profiteroles are great fun to impress friends – but simply remember to bake similar sizes on the same trays, as smaller cakes will obviously cook faster.).

The best temperature is 200ºC (fan 180ºC)/400ºF/gas mark 6, and the pastries will need about 15–20 minutes, depending on their size. They should be well risen and golden. Make sure they are nice and dry in the centre too, which is most important if you are going to fill them with cream.

Fill these buns with whipped cream or crème pâtissière (see page 57). They are good dipped in melted chocolate, or with melted chocolate or fondant icing poured over the top.

1

2

3

4

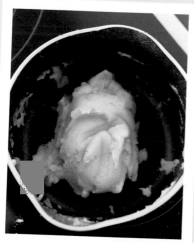

5

6

Sweet shortcrust pastry

This pastry – known in France as pâte sucrée – is perfect for lining tart bases and using as a topping for sweet pies.

Makes 250g (9oz)

Preparation time: 20–30 minutes,
  + chilling
Cooking time: 15–20 minutes

115g (4oz) plain flour, plus extra
  for dusting
50g (2oz) cold unsalted butter, cut into
  small pieces, plus extra for greasing
25g (1oz) icing sugar, sifted
1 egg yolk
1 tsp vanilla extract

Sift the flour into a mixing bowl. Add the measured butter and rub in with your fingertips until the mixture resembles fine breadcrumbs. Stir in the sugar. Make a well in the centre.

Lightly beat the egg yolk with 1 tbsp cold water and the vanilla extract. Add to the well in the flour mixture and mix in with your fingertips. Gather together to make a soft dough. Wrap in clingfilm and chill for an hour before rolling out.

Knead the dough minimally, then roll out on a lightly floured surface until a little larger than a 23cm (9in) loose-bottomed flan tin. Use some extra butter to grease the flan tin, base and sides.

Lift the pastry over the rolling pin, drape in the buttered tin and press over the base and up the side. Trim the excess pastry by by rolling a rolling pin across the top. Prick the base of the pastry with a fork.

Blind-baking: Line the raw pastry case with greaseproof paper and fill to the top with ceramic baking beans (they conduct more heat than the dried beans often recommended). Bake in an oven preheated to 200°C (fan 180°C)/400°F/gas mark 6 for 10 minutes until the pastry is golden brown. Remove the baking beans and paper, and put the pastry case back in the oven for 5–10 minutes to dry out the base.

If you are using the base for liquid mixture, brush the inside of the case with egg-wash (a beaten egg mixed with 1 tbsp milk) after taking out the baking beans, and cook for 10 minutes to seal the tart and keep the crunchiness longer. Another way to keep the tart nice and crunchy is to brush melted white or dark chocolate on the inside of the baked tart; leave to set before adding the filling.

Alternatives

Almond shortcrust: replace 30g (1¼oz) of the flour with ground almonds (or ground roasted hazelnuts or walnuts).

Chocolate shortcrust: replace 30g (1¼oz) of the flour with sifted pure cocoa powder.

Tip

If you are not very good at rolling pastry and lining flan tins, roll the pastry on a sheet of clingfilm slightly dusted with flour. Just lift the film and turn over on to the ring. Press down and gently remove the film (see opposite). Don't worry if bits break off the sheet of pastry when you put it in your pie dish; you can simply patch and press it together.

1

2

3

4

5

6

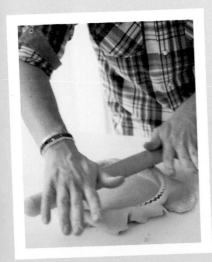

7

8

9

Shortbread

This is the perfect recipe for making delicious buttery biscuits and cookies, the ground rice giving a nice texture. You can cut the biscuits into different shapes using cookie cutters, and they can also be rolled very thinly to layer with cream and fruit for desserts. You could even make 'stained-glass' vitraille biscuits (see below). Try adding finely grated orange or lemon zest or ground hazelnuts too.

Makes about 16 plain or 24 vitraille biscuits
Preparation time: 20 minutes, + chilling
Cooking time: 8–10 minutes

100g (3½oz) unsalted butter, at room temperature, plus extra for greasing
50g (2oz) caster sugar, plus extra for sprinkling
1 tsp vanilla extract
175g (6oz) self-raising flour, plus extra for dusting
2 tsp fine ground rice, plus extra for sprinkling

Cream the butter, sugar and vanilla together in a bowl, using an electric hand whisk, until almost white. Sift in the measured flour and ground rice. Combine using your fingertips. Don't over-mix!

Squeeze the mixture into a ball and wrap in clingfilm. Leave to rest in the fridge for at least an hour.

Preheat the oven to 170°C (fan 150°C)/325°F/gas mark 3. Grease non-stick baking sheets with extra butter, or line with baking paper.

Roll the dough out on a lightly floured surface until 5mm (¼in) thick, and cut out shapes with cutters. As you go along, squeeze the trimmings together – although try to not over-work the dough – and continue rolling and cutting shapes until all the dough is used up. Place the biscuits on the prepared baking sheets.

For simple shortbread, sprinkle the biscuits with some caster sugar and fine ground rice before baking in the preheated oven for 8–10 minutes. Once cooked, allow to cool on the baking sheets.

Alternatives

Vitraille shortbread: Make and roll the shortbread dough as above. Cut your biscuits into hearts or other shapes, and using a smaller cutter in the same shape (or different), cut out the centre. Place the shapes on a baking tray lined with baking paper, and place an old-fashioned coloured boiled sweet in the hole (make sure the hole is larger than the sweet or it will boil over the edge and spoil the effect). During cooking the sweet will melt, and when cold will set to give the stained-glass effect. Keep an eye on the biscuits as they cook, and remove from the oven as soon as they are golden and the sweet has just melted.

Shortbread biscuits for hanging: For biscuits to hang, cut a hole large enough to pass a ribbon through immediately after the biscuits come out of the oven, while they are still slightly soft.

Tip

It is important not to overwork the shortbread, or it won't be crumbly and short. And be sure to prick the shortbread with a fork before baking it, or it won't be flat when cooked.

Gingerbread biscuits

These biscuits have a wonderful spicy baking smell that will permeate every room of your house. They make good Christmas presents, so you could double the recipe if you liked.

Makes 30 x 7.5cm (3in) biscuits
Preparation time: 20 minutes, + chilling
Cooking time: 10–12 minutes

225g (8oz) plain flour
1 tsp baking powder
2 tsp ground ginger
¾ tsp ground cinnamon
a tiny pinch each of cayenne pepper
    and fine salt
125g (4½oz) unsalted butter, at room
    temperature, cut into small pieces,
    plus extra for greasing
200g (7oz) dark brown caster sugar
2 tbsp golden syrup
1 large egg

Sift the flour, baking powder, ginger, cinnamon, cayenne and salt into a large mixing bowl. Add the measured butter and the sugar and rub the butter with your fingertips until it is absorbed and the mixture has a sandy texture.

Gently beat the egg. Mix in the syrup using a wooden spoon, and gradually add enough of the beaten egg to make a fairly stiff, smooth dough. Shape the dough into a ball and wrap in clingfilm. Place the dough in the fridge to firm up for at least 1 hour.

Preheat the oven to 180°C (fan 160°C)/350°F/gas mark 4 and grease a couple of non-stick baking sheets with extra butter.

Roll out the dough to 5mm (¼in) thickness. Cut the biscuits into your desired shapes and place on the prepared baking sheets.

Bake in the preheated oven for 10–12 minutes until golden brown. (If you want them to hang on a Christmas tree, make holes for the ribbon immediately the biscuits come out of the oven, while they are still hot and soft.) Cool for 2–3 minutes, then loosen with a palette knife and set aside to cool on the baking sheets.

Decorate the biscuits with piped coloured royal icing (see below).

Royal icing

Use British Lion Standard egg whites. If you are worried about using raw eggs, you can buy reconstituted albumen powder instead.

Makes 500g (1lb 2oz)
2 egg whites
1 tsp lemon juice
about 500g (1lb 2oz) icing sugar, sifted
edible food colouring paste (optional)

Tip the egg whites into a bowl and stir in the lemon juice. Gradually add the sieved icing sugar, mixing well after each addition.

Continue adding small amounts of icing sugar until you achieve the desired consistency. For piping, the icing should be fairly stiff.

Edible food colouring paste is highly concentrated, so only use a tiny amount. Dip a cocktail stick into the colouring paste. Mix well before adding more colouring paste to avoid streaks.

Chocolate chip cookies

These sweet cookies, and their many variations, always remind me of my first trip to the USA, where they sell them everywhere straight from the oven…

Makes about 20
Preparation time: 20–30 minutes
Cooking time: 15–17 minutes

175g (6oz) unsalted butter, melted, plus
   extra for greasing
250g (9oz) plain flour
½ tsp bicarbonate of soda
½ tsp salt
200g (7oz) soft dark brown sugar
100g (3½oz) caster sugar
2 tsp vanilla extract
1 egg
1 egg yolk
3 x 100g bags dark chocolate chips

Preheat the oven to 170ºC (fan 150ºC)/325ºF/gas mark 3. Grease two baking trays with extra butter or line with baking paper.

Sift the flour, bicarbonate of soda and salt into a large bowl. Set aside.

Cream the melted butter, brown sugar and caster sugar together in a medium bowl, using an electric hand whisk, until well blended. Beat in the vanilla, egg and egg yolk until light and creamy. Add to the sifted ingredients and mix until just blended. Stir in the chocolate chips by hand, using a wooden spoon.

Drop the dough on to the prepared baking trays - each cookie should be around 2 tablespoons of dough. Do not flatten the dough, as the cookies will do that by themselves, so leave a little space around each for them to spread.

Bake in the preheated oven for 15–17 minutes or until the edges are lightly golden. Cool on the baking trays for a few minutes before transferring to wire racks to cool completely.

Alternatives

Double chocolate cookies: replace 50g (2oz) of the flour with sifted pure cocoa powder.

Macadamia cookies: add 100g (3½oz) chopped macadamia nuts and replace the dark chocolate with 125g (4½oz) white chocolate chips.

Christmas cookies: replace the chocolate chips with 175g (6oz) rolled oats and 125g (4½oz) chopped dried cranberries, and add 1 teaspoon ground cinnamon.

Banana cookies: add 1 mashed really ripe banana to the mixture and replace half the chocolate chips with rolled oats.

Coconut cookies: replace half the chocolate chips with desiccated coconut, for this amazing 'Bounty' cookie.

Peanut butter cookies: Make the basic dough up to the egg and egg yolk stage, omitting the vanilla, then mix in 150g (5oz) chunky peanut butter and 150g (5oz) chopped walnuts, followed by the sifted ingredients. As the cookies come out of the oven, drizzle some clear honey over them – the ultimate indulgence!

Tip

I use an ice-cream scoop to measure my cookie dough out on to the baking sheets, so that they are all the same size.

1

2

3

4

5

6

7

8

9

Index

Acknowledgements

My first thank you goes to the lovely Angela Boggiano, who pushed me to sharpen my pencils and start writing this book. Thank you also to Becca from Mitchell Beazley, for approaching me and looking after me right through this exciting journey – I can't wait for that promised dancing session! We managed to get a great team together. Thanks to the talented Craig and his ever-funny assistant Colin, who made my creations look so yummy on paper. Thanks also to Juliette and Morag – you did a brilliant job at styling this book. Rachel was a great help, as she was for my TV series 'Glamour Puds'; she went out of her way to assist me with all the recipes – we had such a good laugh and thank you for teaching me how to make a cracking cucumber G&T! George, you amazed me! On top of dealing with the shoot, checking recipes, chasing me for quotes and putting the book together, you managed not just to organise your wedding but also to get married and be back at work to finish this project before leaving for your honeymoon. And Susan, thank you for your keen eye and your way with words. We all deserve to enjoy that glass of Champagne! Thank you too to my agent, Anne Kibbel, Jean Egbunike, Fiona Smith and to my team at Cake Boy for their hard work and for sharing my excitement.

Dedication

To Paul and Bobbycat, thank you for having been patient at home – and I hope you enjoyed the leftovers.